Rizzoli
NEW YORK

cruise

Identity, Design and Culture

Peter Quartermaine & Bruce Peter

First published in the United States of America in 2006 by

RIZZOLI NEW YORK

Rizzoli International Publications, Inc.
300 Park Avenue South
New York, NY 10010
www.rizzoliusa.com

Originally published in the United Kingdom in 2006 by

LAURENCE KING

Laurence King Publishing Ltd
71 Great Russell Street
London WC1B 3BN
www.laurenceking.co.uk

Text copyright © 2006 Peter Quartermaine & Bruce Peter

This book was designed and produced by Laurence King Publishing Ltd, London

2006 2007 2008 2009 2010 / 10
9 8 7 6 5 4 3 2 1

Printed in Singapore

ISBN: 0-8478-2796-8

Library of Congress Control Number: 2005929975

FRONTISPIECE The magically luminous world of the ship; Orient Line's 1951 *Oronsay* in port at night, with posed figures. Romance under the stars, the handrails, stairways and tiered decks, glimpses of an immaculately painted and maintained structure with a humming life all its own – these are all part of the thrill of being aboard ship.

PAGES 2–3 Cunard's liner, *Queen Elizabeth*, made her maiden voyage in 1940 as a troop ship. She did not carry passengers until 1946, plying the Southampton to New York route. British service and style on board were legendary, and with her restrained superstructure and grand funnels she still epitomizes the 'classic' passenger ship. Though her own success at cruising from the 1960s was limited, many modern vessels still aspire to emulate her aura of timeless elegance. Her elder sister, *Queen Mary*, is preserved at Long Beach, California

The ship is – and has always been – the largest human construction capable of casting off and moving across the globe. Most of our planet is made up of ocean, and migration across water has been a defining part of the history of humankind. Today, we no longer voyage in search of uncharted territories to colonize, but the uncontested efficiency of maritime transport underpins the global economy as never before: a ship needs neither wings nor wheels, and the sea no maintenance. In its design, every ship – including every cruise ship – is a compromise between the optimum demands of trade (profit) and the minimum requirements of survival (safety). A cruise ship, however, must also be fun and, for its passengers, understandably remains primarily a hotel and entertainment venue that moves. To design, construct and operate such complex floating cities demands imagination, technical expertise – and materials – of the very highest order. The unique achievements of cruise ships in satisfying all these demands through their architecture and design have hitherto been largely overlooked; in this respect, as in others, the sea remains another world. This book seeks to rectify this omission by exploring and illustrating the identity, design and culture of the cruise companies and their ships. In recording the changing tastes of cruise passengers themselves that have driven the corporate response, it also celebrates what is a rapidly growing and culturally significant phenomenon.

Introduction

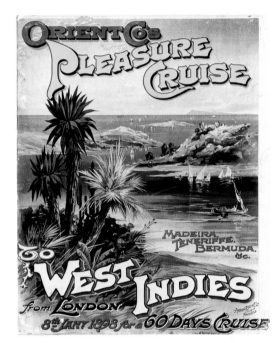

Leisure is more than the time that you can spend as you like, it has become an omnipresent culture of fun with enormous economic importance. Our social identity is determined by the way we spend our leisure at least as much as by the work we do or the possessions we own.

Tracy Metz, *Fun! Leisure and Landscape*, 2002

The cruise business is growing rapidly year on year, and some ten million passengers will cruise during 2005 in the United States alone, and around eleven million worldwide. Everywhere, from Alaska to Ancona, from Plymouth to Perth, and from Valletta to Venice, cruising is the boom leisure scene that provides new life for moribund ports and their hinterland, and recruits staff worldwide for its ever-larger ships.

Cruise statistics are oceanic in scale. Lead company Carnival reported a net income of US $294 million for the last quarter of 2004, up 43 percent; Norwegian Cruise Line is to spend US $1 billion on two new ships for 2007; Royal Caribbean Cruises Limited declared an increased income of 69 percent, at US $474.4 million, for 2004. Advance booking on P&O Cruises' new flagship, *Arcadia*, reached 78 percent while the vessel was still being built in Italy. People just can't wait, it seems, to go to sea.

Ashore things are changing just as quickly. Kochi (formerly Cochin) is investing US $22.7 billion to become India's global hub port; Miami is building a new cruise terminal and saw 3.5 million passengers in 2004 (and rising); New York is investing US$ 30 million on a modern cruise facility in Brooklyn, while Genting Bhd, the Malaysian owner of Star Cruises, is considering putting US $1 billion into a Singapore cruise terminal.

ABOVE Together with the Mediterranean, the Caribbean was an early favourite destination for cruise ships, and the fascination of its climate, vegetation and varied cultures still holds today. This 1898 poster promotes sixty-day cruises to a beautiful location that today's cruise industry places at increasing risk.

FACING The final step from the gangway onto the deck of the ship takes a passenger into a different world. The culture of normal life is cast off, as the ship itself shapes the daily routine. Here, a passenger returns to Orient Line's 1951 *Oronsay* berthed at Naples that same year. The passenger terminal for liners was built during the fascist era to serve emigration to north and south America, but has since been refurbished to assume a new life as a cruise terminal.

Conte BIANCAMANO

La Prima Classe

"ITALIA"

ABOVE The *Conte Biancamano* was launched at Dalmuir, Scotland, in 1925, when the Clyde led the world in shipbuilding. Her interior decor was partly executed by Italian craftsmen who travelled to the yard. One Italian firm involved still works on cruise ships, and also recently recreated the plasterwork for La Fenice in Venice, after that theatre was destroyed by fire.

FACING A cruise ship can dwarf a port. As built, P&O's classic 1953 *Arcadia*, here moored at Pago-Pago, Samoa, in 1966, carried 679 first-class and 735 tourist-class passengers (roughly equivalent to the crew of a large cruise ship today) and was noted for her 'very cosy, club-like atmosphere'. *Arcadia* was built for the Australia and Far East run, but later turned to cruising. Her innovative observation lounge, whose large windows are visible here below her bridge, was a real asset in this new role.

A swelling sea of paperback guides and weekend press supplements reflect the evident popularity of cruising, but this book is the first critical, though affectionate, look at a quite extraordinary economic, cultural and design phenomenon that began to employ mass-market, purpose-built vessels only from the early 1970s. It is all the more remarkable in an age that has largely forgotten the sea as a means of travel and transport: we travel internationally by air, while containers render our goods anonymous, and their dedicated ports are remote and uninteresting. At the same time, once-bustling city wharves now merit tourist signs as 'historic wharves' – meaning dead port areas. Few people today are now familiar with any ocean-going ship other than a cruise vessel or a ferry, yet they are more likely to have been on a cruise than previous generations were to have experienced oceanic passenger travel. In cultural terms, the design and decor of cruise ships reflect and shape our expectations of the seagoing experience in novel and revealing ways; floating cities in conception, these mega-vessels, together with their passengers and crews, mirror the priorities of our more mundane terrestrial worlds – for better and for worse.

A cruise ship is a large passenger vessel whose voyages are driven not by the demands of enterprise, but of entertainment. Where passenger liners of an earlier period provided scheduled transport services around the globe, cruise ships mostly ply a relatively limited number of routes. Most importantly, it is the voyage itself – and especially the extensive onboard leisure and entertainment facilities of the ship itself – that attract today's cruise passengers. The ship is the thing that defines this experience of a voyage from A to B, and back again.

To design, construct and operate a modern cruise ship demands daunting talents and funds, but these vessels are mostly popular in their target market, style and function – a fact that may explain

their neglect by commentators on architecture and design. Most readily available guides omit ships altogether apart from well-worn references to the interiors of the *Queen Mary* or *Normandie* as examples of art deco. For most critics, it seems, ship design stopped in the 1930s, yet passenger vessels today are the largest, the most expensive (at almost US $400 million each), and certainly the most complex – and popular – ever built. Indeed, despite innumerable book titles to the contrary, *this* is the 'golden age of cruising', and the ships that make that experience possible for more people than ever before warrant better appreciation. A significant element of contemporary leisure culture, they also raise post-colonial issues in both their crewing and in their impact on the locations they visit. Above all, they transport millions of us across this globalized and troubled world to encounter, however briefly, peoples and places different from our own.

Cruise ships and their vacationing cargoes are by no means always welcome. Several destinations have sought to regulate, even block, ship visits, but vessels pay a fee per passenger, and this, together with port dues and passenger spending, is a powerful persuader. Passenger vessels have long been seen, by their home nations and by those whose shores they visit, as agents of power and influence. Cruise ships are but the latest in many such armadas, though they come bearing dollars rather than seeking gold. For the passenger (or 'guest' as the industry now terms it), a cruise is something of a contradiction – it is that voyage from A to B and back again, but with the appeal of sunshine, indulgence and the exotic, and often a hint of sexual liberation. 'Size matters,' asserts one brochure – referring to the tonnage of the ship, of course. The style and tone of cruise publicity is calculatedly relaxing and carefree. Its emphasis is on getting away from it all on weekend cruises, world cruises, adventure cruises, discovery cruises, speciality 'themed' cruises – or on any number of private charter

cruises booked by employers, universities, clubs and interest groups. In Britain, Saga specializes in cruises for the older generation, while Ocean Village Holidays bills itself as 'The cruise line for people who don't do cruises'.

Destinations range from Alaska to Antarctica, and duration from a three-day hop from Miami to Nassau and back, to round-the-world cruises lasting three months and costing £40,000 (US $70,000) or more. Cruising is big business – and needs big ships. The largest vessels launching in 2005 will carry some 3,000 passengers served by more than 1,000 crew. Support staff and technology ashore is equally formidable, from company-owned recruitment agencies, and training schools for officers, chefs, waiters and cabin staff, to commercial dry docks that can cut a ship in two and insert a completely finished new section. Spares are stocked at strategic locations around the world. Companies are planning ever-larger ships, and in early 2005 shipyards had orders for twenty-three vessels for a total value of more than US $11 billion, with Italian shipyards by far the most productive. Carnival's 'Pinnacle Project' for the largest-ever cruise ship, at a cost of more than US $1 billion, was under detailed discussion with Italian shipbuilders Fincantieri.

People who would never have considered it, even a few years ago, are now cruising; yet still only one-third of those who take a holiday take a cruise, and the cruise companies' aim is to get the remainder on board. However, even at present growth rates, existing cruise ports may become so crowded that future generations of even larger liners will sail to at least some newly constructed destinations. Visiting such passenger versions of container terminals may not be everyone's idea of a cruise, but back in the 1960s, passenger ships of all kinds seemed doomed to history by cheap and fast 'jetliners'. So how, and why, has such an extraordinary revival come about?

ABOVE Shore visits are an important aspect of any cruise (though some passengers prefer to stay on board the ship). Passengers from the United States generally prefer a different shore visit each day, whereas the British quite enjoy a day or two at sea. Here, passengers disembark from Orient Line's *Oronsay* in 1951. Modern vessels avoid the need for such a steep gangway from the deck by using a passenger access door low down in the hull.

FACING A ship is a strictly hierarchical community; at sea, a captain has sweeping powers. Crew uniforms denote rank by braided bands on jacket cuffs, and other insignia. Here officers sport 'tropical whites' as they demonstrate the use of sextants. Such traditional instruments would still be needed to establish the ship's position should electronic other navigational equipment fail. This is also Orient Line's 1951 *Oronsay*; her 'Welsh bonnet' funnel extension helped lift engine smuts clear.

ABOVE Cruises to ice regions are increasingly popular, but there is also concern over the threat they may pose to such formerly remote areas. Not all local residents are enthusiastic, either. The thrill for passengers of seeing glaciers close to is obvious from this shot on the foredeck of the 1949 *Oslofjord*. She carried a maximum of 646 passengers, with a high level of provision in both tourist- and first-, but cruised as a one-class vessel.

FACING P&O Cruises' 2002 *Oceana* (built 2000, as *Ocean Princess*) poses in the Caribbean. An idyllic image, but when even one cruise ship drops anchor offshore, beaches can be invaded by several thousand people. If two or three arrive, some 9,000 passengers may be looking for a shady palm tree. As a result, some cruise companies now lease or buy beach areas – sometimes complete islands – for the exclusive use of their passengers.

The company that best exemplifies the startling development of cruising over the past thirty years is Carnival Corporation, the world's largest and most successful cruise company, based in Miami, Florida – which is itself the undisputed cruise capital of the world. Carnival was founded in 1972 by Ted Arison, an entrepreneur from Israel. Arison had initially chartered an Israeli car ferry, the *Nili*, to carry freight trailers and cruise passengers on routes from Miami to Port-Au-Prince in Haiti and Montego Bay in Jamaica; the *Nili* had previously plied this route for the Pan American Cruise Line, founded by ex-hotelier Ed Stephan. Despite the limited charms of these freight-orientated ports, the venture proved successful, but *Nili*'s owner went bankrupt and the ship was arrested. Faced with the dilemma of eager passengers but no ship, Arison struck a deal with the Norwegian ship-owner Knut Kloster, who had built a similarly well-appointed ferry, the *Sunward*, to carry British tourists from Southampton to Spain's Algarve and Costa del Sol via Lisbon and Gibraltar. This plan also came to nothing, as General Franco closed Spain's border with the British enclave, so yet another idea was needed. Kloster had been approached by Stephan about the possibility of sending the *Sunward* to Miami, but when they failed to agree terms he instead formed the Norwegian Caribbean Line in partnership with Arison.

After a slow start, the venture prospered but, following differences with Kloster, Arison went his own way and founded Carnival. His challenging start in cruise ships was to stand Arison in good stead; he acquired invaluable knowledge of the market (and of ship operation) the hard way, and this experience was to inform a series of high-risk but successful decisions. From modest beginnings with one converted transatlantic liner, the *Mardi Gras* (formerly the 1960 Canadian Pacific liner *Empress of Britain*), Carnival has since absorbed many of the world's most famous passenger shipping lines, and

now comprises some twenty companies, while its own Miami-based fleet totals twelve vessels, built mainly since the mid-1990s. Another twelve ships are on order. Carnival Corporation is now steered by Ted Arison's son, Micky, and owns companies that include Italian firm Costa Cruises, Britain's Cunard, Ocean Village, P&O Cruises and Swan Hellenic, and the American line Princess Cruises, as well as the prestigious Dutch company Holland America Line, the 'super luxury' brand Seabourn, and the adventure-orientated company Windstar. Its success reflects significant changes in cruising since the 1970s from its rather conservative inter-war role – changes that Carnival itself has played a major part in bringing about, especially in the design and marketing of cruise ships themselves.

Modern cruising, as we know it today, began in the United States, thanks to new ideas by outsiders just like Arison. These individuals saw the opportunity to run elderly ships (registered outside the United States for financial reasons) on cheap-and-cheerful jaunts from sunny Florida ports to Nassau in the Bahamas. Among the first was Eastern Shipping Corporation which, in 1947, ran the *Nuevo Dominico* from Miami. Seven years later, the company acquired the elderly coastal liners, *Yarmouth* and *Evangeline*, the latter vessel subsequently passing to Stephan's Yarmouth Cruise Lines. Yarmouth added the *Yarmouth Castle* to its fleet, while Eastern purchased *Bahama Star* in 1959 and *Ariadne* in 1961. Most of these steamers were well past their prime, and several even had wooden deckhouses. In 1965, the *Yarmouth Castle* burned from stem to stern, and a year later the Norwegian-owned *Viking Princess* burned out while sailing from Miami to Curaçao. Ironically, the American authorities had introduced the world's strictest fire regulations for ships registered in the United States after a fire on the coastal liner *Morro Castle* in 1934, and they now actively discouraged elderly, foreign-flagged vessels from American waters. Stephan, for example, went on to found Pan American Cruises,

ABOVE The pioneering cruise ship *Yarmouth*, built 1927, captured against the 1950s Nassau waterfront, when this harbour town was still a working local port rather than a 'cruise destination'. Today, the trading craft and sacks of produce are gone; local people sell 'traditional wares' (manufactured for the purpose) to passengers from the cruise ships, or provide other tourist-related services. The *Yarmouth* carried some 350 passengers.

FACING A study of Orient Line's 1948 *Orcades* leaving Sydney's Pyrmont wharf for 'the old country'. Departing passengers threw streamers to friends and relatives on the quayside, both parties holding them until they finally parted.

Commodore Cruise Line and Royal Caribbean in Florida – but using all-modern tonnage of innovative design.

As in many other fields, developments in design and technology profoundly influenced the nature of cruising. Before jet travel, southern Florida was remote, even for most Americans; reaching Miami meant a possibly stormy two-day voyage from New York, or a long car drive. A rapidly expanding domestic air network in the United States brought passengers to the ships *en masse*. While international jet travel made many relatively modern passenger liners redundant, it also introduced 'fly-cruise' packages from hub ports. Many surplus ships were cheaply and imaginatively converted for Caribbean and Mediterranean cruising, and Miami became America's 'gateway to the Caribbean', with ever-larger vessels meeting the growing demand. In a virtuous circle, these larger ships brought economies of scale, and cruising became more widely affordable. The vast populous of middle America, many of whom had never seen the sea, much less a large passenger ship, began to book cruises. It was a key shift, but what middle America wanted was neither the lofty saloons and stuffy silver service of Britain's old-world Cunard, nor the continental exoticism of the Italian Line or North German Lloyd. These new cruise passengers had to be tempted away from their familiar theme parks and hotels by an informal cruise experience carefully designed and marketed as different – but not *too* different. Unsurprisingly, the mass-market cruise ship would owe much in its design and ambience to elements of the hotel resort, the entertainment strip and the shopping mall.

To offer the sophisticated and varied experiences demanded by today's passengers, cruise ships have become technologically advanced leisure and entertainment sites, with facilities rivalling Vegas-style venues. Micky Arison points out that it is a mistake to see Carnival as being in the business of

ABOVE Increasingly, passengers wish to use internet facilities, and the 2004 *Carnival Valor* is fully 'wi-fi', equipped for wire-free computer use. Where once passengers communicated by postcard when in port, nowadays to cruise no longer means forgoing the dubious pleasures of email and internet banking.

ABOVE LEFT Modern ships recruit high-quality entertainers worldwide as part of the varied cruise experience they offer. In addition to the Show Lounge, *Carnival Spirit* has eight entertainment venues offering guests different styles of entertainment, plus 'Fun Features' that, Carnival boasts, include 'The Jungle, Deco Lounge, Techno Arcade, Conference Room, The Chapel, Chippendale Library and Internet Café, and Fashion Boulevard'.

FACING The Nouveau Supper Club on *Carnival Spirit* exploits the unusual space under her glazed funnel area to great effect. For an extra charge, guests can book at the Club for gourmet meals and five-star service. The whole ambience, including the spectacular curving staircase, is designed as a flattering setting for any passenger who wishes to be a VIP for the evening.

Boy's Own

PAPER

IN THIS ISSUE

Liners of Tomorrow

LAURENCE DUNN

shipping: 'We're not shipping, we're tourism.' The voyage itself and the exotic interest of ports of call were once the main attraction, but cruise ships now compete directly with shore-based vacation and leisure sites: Arison points out that 'if our cruises get too expensive, our customers will go to a hotel'. Despite globalization, significant national differences remain: British cruise passengers still generally prefer to stay longer at sea than their American counterparts, who like to stop at a port each day, while karaoke and family rooms are especially important for Star Cruises. What all cruise ships have in common is that ports of call are now little more than extras along the way; the ship itself is the destination that sells the cruise, and is designed, promoted and operated accordingly.

Commercial opportunity and keen competition will ensure that cruise ships develop as rapidly over the next thirty-five years as they have since the launch in 1968 of *Skyward*, the first purpose-built modern cruise ship. If so, then ship designers face unparalleled challenges – and passengers quite extraordinary delights. There could be problems, too: increasingly large and glamorous cruise developments in poor countries bring income to some, but frustration for all those beyond the security fencing. Cruise ships are the tinsel-town followers, to some extent also the inheritors, of historically complex maritime trades and traditions. In shaping its future roles in the light of these, the cruise industry may yet need ideas more original than anything we have seen to date.

ABOVE An impression by the eminent marine artist Laurence Dunn of the transatlantic liner *France*, then being built at St Nazaire. In the 1950s, popular British magazines such as *Boy's Own Paper* often featured ships as part of national culture in a way that now seems unthinkable. Interestingly, Dunn's article on liners in this issue (which survived the rigours of a lending library) noted that 'unless air travel can be made much cheaper' they would 'still carry the bulk of the world's travellers'. It was, and they didn't – but people did start cruising.

FACING For publicity purposes, aerial photography is often used to convey a sense of the ship's power and serenity. Here, the stern pool area and tiered decks on P&O's 1995 *Oriana* are shown to advantage as she sails into the sunset. The self-contained quality of the cruise ship is dramatically emphasized, but deck layout is also clearly displayed.

History and Culture

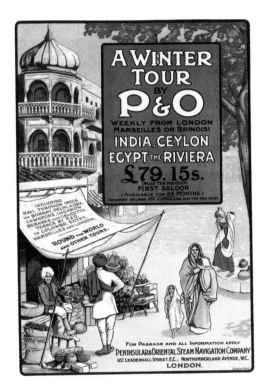

Modern cruising must be understood historically in the context of its natural element – the sea. Yet, in many ways, the very notion of 'cruising' runs counter to any traditional role of the sea and seafaring in history, literature or art. Traditionally, to 'go to sea' was both unpleasant and dangerous, a considerable and calculated risk taken only for such compelling reasons as fishing, trade, essential travel – or escape from poverty or persecution. These last motives still apply today: the lower ranks of the world's merchant navies are largely crewed from poor countries, while refugees and economic migrants perish at sea with dreadful regularity just off the tourist beaches of southern Spain and Italy, and elsewhere.

For most seafarers life at sea, especially in the so-called 'golden age of sail', was harsh. Prior to the iron steamships built from the 1860s, most vessels were tiny by modern standards, and sheer lack of space precluded comfort for either passengers or crew. Yet most international travel was by ship, and journeys even within large continents or countries were often made between river or sea ports; even today, the locations of Australia's major cities (with the exception of the later capital, Canberra) reflect this. Ports have unique national and international significance, and the current redevelopment of many to provide cruise terminals is but the latest phase of their special history.

No cultural attitude has changed more dramatically than the way we regard the ocean and its margins. Our seemingly instinctive cult of the sea, and of 'the seaside', as a location for healthy recreation in fact dates only from the latter half of the eighteenth century, and mass tourism came largely from the mobility that ordinary people gained from developments in transport technology – notably the steam train (and later the boom in private car ownership). By the second half of the nineteenth century, local pleasure steamers offered a marine leisure experience, their routes often

ABOVE A 1953 brochure for three vessels operated by American Grace Line to the Caribbean, South America, and destinations through the Panama Canal. The dining room on each was 'high up' (bad in rough weather) and featured 'wide casement windows which open direct onto promenade decks', while 'ceilings roll back so you may dine under the stars' – though here the ship's funnel obtrudes. Classical elegance is the keynote here, while the painting of a sailing vessel adds a discreet maritime touch.

complementing the services of expanding regional railway companies (which sometimes operated the ships, too). An intrinsic part of the 'pleasure' such domesticated sea travel offered was that passengers never really lost sight of land. The ships themselves reflected this, elegantly decorated as they often were in a manner reminiscent of pier and promenade architecture ashore: Edwardian coastal pleasure steamers had low, large open decks, boasted gilded scrollwork on the bows and paddle boxes, and offered ornate passenger saloons. Onboard entertainment even had an 'exotic' touch, with the grandest British vessels often hiring German musicians to serenade their passengers – the very height of fashion.

By 1937, the British company Coast Lines Limited, which also operated extensive short sea cargo services, was offering 'Cruises to Scottish Firths and Fjords' in its twin-funnelled steam yacht *Killarney* from Whitsun until mid-September: 'She provides all the comforts of a private yacht and you feel that she is something more than the ship on which you happen to be travelling, that she belongs to you and is your home.' The company noted coyly that a successful holiday depended on 'food and exercise', and that on a *Killarney* cruise 'the bracing sea air' supplied the appetite, while the cuisine itself was 'perfect'. These were definitely not sunshine cruises.

Such summertime coastal trips were essentially a diversion – much as cruising is today – and illustrate how increasing social mobility and technological advances change the very nature of travel. Comfort, enhanced by a range of services, is among the most significant of these changes that we now take largely for granted. We travel for business or pleasure cocooned in vehicles that move us rapidly from place to place: plush automobiles, luxury coaches, fast aeroplanes and air-conditioned trains with dining cars and flush toilets. In 1840s Britain it was railway tunnels and viaducts that, for the

ABOVE This illustration, by the Austrian artist Franz Lenhart, promotes a spring cruise in 1934 (year XII of the fascist calendar). This cruise was outward on the 1928 Cosulich Line *Vulcania*, returning on her sister ship *Saturnia*. Ports from Gibraltar to Port Said were visited on cruises lasting from two weeks to a month. The ships were equipped with powerful transmitters for sending 'Marconigrammes' to any Italian receiving station, which could then forward passengers' messages worldwide.

ABOVE LEFT For the fortunate few, travelling to work could be as good as a cruise: the 1928 *Leopoldville* sailed for the Compagnie Belge Maritime du Congo between Antwerp and the Belgian colony, whose brutal imperial regime had inspired Joseph Conrad's 1902 novella, *Heart of Darkness*. This publicity image emphasizes the vessel's technological prowess, and her hull dominates the flanking continents of Europe and Africa.

ABOVE The deck pool on the 1932 *Conte di Savoia*, from material advertising a cruise in the eastern Mediterranean. Italian passenger vessels of this period were very advanced technologically, and facilities for passengers were also of a high standard.

ABOVE RIGHT In this image from the 1930s, Italian passengers make the most of sunshine on deck. The jackets – and socks – suggest that this may be a spring or autumn cruise.

RIGHT This 1934 cruise map of the Mediterranean is for a spring cruise to the eastern Mediterranean by the Italian cruise ship *Roma*: 'Three continents, four civilizations: the classical and the Christian; the Islamic and the modern. All the riches of history; a compendium of culture.'

FACING This brochure cover, from the same year and for the same Italian shipping company, highlights the perennial appeal of foreign cultures ashore rather than of breezy life on the ship's deck. Historically, Italy had close connections with many Arab countries, and this tradition is continued today in, for example, long-term energy contracts with Libya.

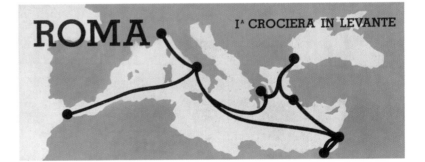

ABOVE In a carefully posed shot of the tourist-class lounge on P&O's 1937 *Stratheden*, social life on board is presented as quietly genteel rather than luxurious, though the architectural spaces are clean in decor and well-lit. Built for the UK–India–Australia service, *Stratheden* was later used for cruising and in 1946, after a stint as a troop ship, she was the first P&O vessel to resume passenger service, following a ten-month reconversion.

FACING TOP At the time of this picture, 1953, Grace Line was a pioneer in cruises to the Caribbean. State rooms such as this one were 'full outside', and each had 'a private, fresh-water shower or tub bath with shower'. All passenger accommodation (as on many American vessels) was ahead of the time in being fully air-conditioned. There was also 'a telephone in every room', though the rather staid furniture and decor here do not square with the emphasis on modern technology.

FACING BELOW Illustrations by artist Ceri Richards grace a company booklet for the innovative 1935 Orient Line vessel *Orion*. Their restrained and elegant modernism perfectly captures the intended design spirit of the ship itself.

first time, enabled people to be transported almost effortlessly 'through', rather than across, the landscape – an experience that profoundly changed concepts of time and space. (It was the speed of train travel that first necessitated synchronized time across large distances.) At an immediate level, transport infrastructures developed design languages that were both functional and reassuring. Today, 'transit' within predefined zones, rather than 'travel' from place to place in a fully experienced sense, is the norm for most of us. The practice of commuting, born initially of Britain's railway development, and of both industrialization and suburbanization in the second half of the nineteenth century, is now a daily drudge for millions worldwide – and not only in the major cities of the West.

The cruise ship promises exotic and luxurious escape from such tedious routines – not only in its voyaging and destinations, but in its very design and decor. Oddly, though, the international and corporate character of the cruise industry itself replicates those very aspects of modern life from which it promises its guests release. Only detailed planning and massive capital investment makes possible the carefree seagoing vacations that look so tempting in the coloured brochures, or on images from real-time, ship-mounted cameras that can be accessed online. Cruise ships themselves run to very demanding schedules, made possible only by highly professional management and sophisticated technology.

Such intriguing contradictions have their own history. Escapist architecture that celebrates indulgence as a virtue, not a vice, reflects a deep utopian leisure tradition at the very heart of modernity. In his 1946 *Collected Essays*, British writer George Orwell observed of the mid-1930s that the 'modern civilized ... idea of pleasure is already partly attained in the more magnificent dance halls, movie palaces, hotels, restaurants and luxury liners'. He felt that on 'a pleasure cruise or in a Lyons

THE NEW 23,371 TON ORIENT LINER

A ROOM WITH A VIEW

IL PONTE DEGLI SPORTS

OTTE RIVNITE & COSVLICH & LLOYD SABAVDO & NAVIGAZIONE GENE

ABOVE 'Any ocean voyage has glamour ... Add to it those exclusively GRACE Line ports of call whose names alone set the fancy roaming back through the centuries when the New World was writing its first chapters in blood and gold across the turquoise Spanish Main ... and there you have the elements that compose a GRACE Cruise.' 'Outdoor tiled swimming pools' were one of the 'many exclusive features' on the 'splendid liners which were built especially for tropical cruising'. Pools are always a problem, though, and the wave in the background here almost reaches the pool's lip. From a 1953 publicity brochure.

LEFT This rendering of the lido deck on the famous Italian line *Rex*, launched in August 1931, is by Edina and Vittorio Accornero. Artistic licence enlarges the deck space, but certainly captures the grandeur of the ship that two years running won the Blue Riband for the fastest Atlantic crossing. She was sunk by Allied bombing off Capodistria in September 1944.

GRACE LINE

18 Day Cruises to the

CARIBBEAN
SOUTH AMERICA
PANAMA CANAL

in the luxurious

"SANTA ROSA"
"SANTA PAULA"
"SANTA ELENA"

GRACE LINE

Corner House one already gets something more than a glimpse of this future paradise'. The modernistic Lyons Corner House eating places so familiar in Orwell's Britain are themselves now part of urban legend, but the cruise ship has not so much survived as reinvented itself since the 1930s by offering a whole range of 'future paradises' – at sea.

To cruise is to voyage deep sea for pleasure, an aim best achieved in a large and well-appointed ship on a calm and sunny ocean. Even today, most cruising is in temperate climes, and cruise ships have never been larger or more luxurious. No matter how varied and sophisticated the diversions offered on board, any real ship movement will upset most 'guests' – who will abruptly feel very much like passengers. Located conveniently close to those industrialized nations that were at the forefront of ship design and construction in the late nineteenth century, it was the alluring and relatively sheltered waters of the Mediterranean that saw the very earliest cruises.

In 1843, the British Peninsular and Oriental Steam Navigation Company (better known today as the cruise company P&O) sent one of its paddle steamers on a passenger-carrying round trip from London to the Black Sea. The pioneering British travel operator Thomas Cook offered his first commercial cruise to Egypt, the Middle East and Greece in 1894. He also exercised a virtual monopoly on Nile steamers from 1892, and developed a high-quality fleet of these inland cruise vessels, building new ones as recently as the 1980s. In his invaluable 2000 study, *Cruise Ships: An Evolution in Design,* the shipping and design writer Philip Dawson records that in 1896 a ship-owner in grey-skied Hamburg advertised a world voyage in a large sailing vessel with the aims of 'promoting the safety, the comfort, the entertainment and the instruction of the passengers'. In varying degrees, these remain the aims of cruising to this day.

ABOVE This suitably 'exotic' luggage label for P&O services to the British colony of Hong Kong features rendering of a traditional Chinese dragon. Such ideosyncratic expressions of graphic design are now largely gone, though companies still often commission design consultancies to co-ordinate styling for a new ship across a wide range of uniforms, publicity and signage.

LEFT A clever publicity shot makes the best of quite restricted deck space on P&O's 1956 *Chitral* as she sails to Hong Kong, with some 300 passengers but also a considerable amount of cargo. She was built as the Belgian *Jadotville* for service from Antwerp to the Belgian Congo, but after the colony achieved independence in 1960, *Jadotville* was sold to P&O. Following the closure of the Suez Canal in 1967, she was transferred to Australia, operating six-week round 'cruises' from Melbourne to Sydney, Brisbane, Japan and Hong Kong.

FACING An immaculately turned out steward serves refreshments to passengers relaxing on a liferaft aboard P&O's 1961 *Canberra*, whose distinctive superstructure forms the backdrop. Deck stewards on modern cruise ships are often more informal in dress, especially in warm climates. This picture was taken by the ship's photographer in the Mediterranean, en route to Naples, in 1965.

Mass-market cruising, however, promises entertainment, rather than 'instruction' and self-improvement (though possibilities for these are increasing), and passengers are more often the work-weary middle class than those able to afford a latter-day version of the Grand Tour. In 1930, a leaflet for 'Cruises de Luxe to the Mediterranean' was decidedly uplifting: 'Colour – mystery – romance – these you will find on the golden shores of the sunlit Mediterranean … sunny lands and blue waters. Cruise in this luxury dream ship … Gain experience – information – inspiration.' Such phrases are still echoed in publicity for cruises offered by specialized companies catering for self-selecting niche markets, but the mass-market cruise ship differs both from these and the traditional ocean liner, though it shrewdly cultivates the latter's mystique. The design of traditional passenger liners proudly proclaimed not only national identity but also industrial modernity and technological progress. Ironically, it was these last aspects that ensured the demise of such vessels: the famous 1950s Cunard line slogan 'Getting there is half the fun' may have been true, but those who saw 'getting there' as a priority, and had the money, took the fastest ships – and, eventually, jets. Cruising in the hectic twenty-first century is essentially slow-paced, offering the seemingly irresistible allure of comfortable nostalgia spiced with cautious samplings of other cultures. The centre of the cruise experience is the social world of the ship itself, a focus well-captured in Carnival's copyrighted phrase, 'The Fun Ships'.

Cruises were initially expensive and exclusive, and most cruise vessels of the early twentieth century were minute by today's standards, deliberately echoing the elegant lines of royal steam yachts. The 1907 British royal yacht *Alexandra*, commissioned by King Edward VII to bring his Danish wife back across the North Sea, was actually sold in 1925 to a Norwegian company, and henceforth carried one hundred pampered passengers as the luxurious cruise yacht *Prins Olav*.

ABOVE Passengers land on the South Pacific island of Tonga from Orient Line's 1935 *Orion*. She was revolutionary for a large ship in having only one funnel and one mast. Her clean and modernistic interior layout and decor were very different from the frocks seen here. As originally built, *Orion* carried 486 first-class and 653 tourist-class passengers between Britain and Australia, but later cruised. She was scrapped in 1963.

FAR LEFT A brochure from November 1928 advertising the passenger service by Hamburg-America Line to ports in East Asia. European shipping companies often elegantly exploited the visual appeal of foreign parts in their publicity material. Today most publicity images are photographic, but earlier examples used stylized graphic images to great effect.

LEFT This 1935 promotion for P&O 'Round Voyages' to the Far East summed up the very essence of a cruise: 'From start to finish of the voyage you will live in the same ship, with service and accommodation at least equalling those of a luxury hotel, and you will have, besides, the many attractions of life at sea and pleasant interludes at the various ports of call.'

German passenger lines offered worldwide cruises from 1890, and the first purpose-built, ocean-going cruise ship was the German *Prinzessin Victoria Luise* (1900), commissioned by the innovative director of the Hamburg America Line, Albert Ballin. In 1927, the elegant Swedish-built motor cruise ship *Stella Polaris* set new standards, for, despite her steam yacht lines, she was diesel-powered, and her accommodation had forced-air heating and ventilation throughout. It would be decades before many British cruise ships met such high standards. The passengers on early cruise ships were well-heeled and well-educated, and facilities on board assumed a certain self-contented independence, with generous provision for reading and writing. Then as now, classical and biblical antiquities were a great attraction, and a sea voyage to the Middle East and North Africa was far more comfortable (and secure) than travel overland.

Shipping companies quickly exploited the opportunities of cruising, with Britain's Orient Line adapting its *Chimborazo* and *Garonne* in 1889, and P&O offering 'Round the World and Other Tours'; it sent its twenty-three-year-old liner *Rome* cruising as the 'Steam Yacht' *Vectis* from 1904. Between the wars, world passenger traffic at sea grew rapidly, and companies cruised their older ships off-season to gain extra income from these less-competitive vessels. On land, a growing international network of luxury trains to steamer and cruise ports spawned well-appointed hotels for imperial travellers from London to Luxor, and from Brighton to Bombay. Such developments had their effect at sea: American passengers, especially, expected en-suite accommodation, and the shared bathroom facilities on many British vessels proved unacceptable. Catering to such demand, American Matson Lines built its luxurious *Malolo* in 1927 for first-class-only service between San Francisco and Honolulu, although she was refitted in the 1930s to accommodate two classes, like her sisters *Mariposa* and *Monterey*.

ABOVE Passengers return to the *Canberra* in one of her lifeboats after a shore visit to Gibraltar in 1969. For reasons of convenience, safety – and sheer passenger numbers on large vessels – cruise companies now prefer their ships to dock alongside wherever possible, and many ports, Gibraltar included, have constructed dedicated cruise facilities.

SOUVENIR LOG

NORD
DEUTSCHER
LLOYD
BREMEN

The British liners *Queen of Bermuda* and *Monarch of Bermuda*, built in the mid-1930s for a weekly service between New York and Bermuda, also catered to the luxury market. These were ships for beautiful people to live the good life, though most decor and furnishing aboard was rather staid, if well-upholstered. The German liners *Bremen* (1929) and *Europa* (1930) were among the first large ships in a deliberately modern style, with sleek exterior profiles and rational interior design. Visually impressive streamlining is not everything, though, and their much-admired low funnels were later raised by several metres to avoid smuts falling on decks astern. In Britain, interior design 'from the cabin door handles to the lay-out of the public rooms' by the young New Zealand architect Brian O'Rorke for the 1935 Orient liner *Orion* achieved rare practical and aesthetic coherence. Indeed, company director Colin Anderson was a member of the pro-modernist Design and Industries Association, and selected O'Rorke for his innovative ideas. *Orion*'s exterior design avoided dramatic (and technically unnecessary) 'streamlining', though she was unusual in having only a single mast and funnel (the later *Orcades* largely dispensed with ventilators in favour of grouped ventilating louvres).

In appearance *Orion* was severe, though with classically elegant proportions. A contemporary colour brochure, elegantly illustrated by the artist Ceri Richards, described her as: 'The reflection of the age in which she serves the public ... a ship stripped of unwanted frills, beautiful by being fitted to her purpose.' Her accommodation was light, airy and a fine example of modern design adapted to the requirements of shipboard life in both scale and detail. By comparison, Cunard's *Queen Mary*, launched the following year, was largely traditional despite her streamlined 'moderne' interiors with fashionable art deco detailing. The difference between the two ships is not surprising: *Queen Mary* was the subsidized national flagship of the pre-eminent imperial and industrial power (albeit one already in

ABOVE A study of the Main Lounge, the centre of entertainment located on the promenade deck, on Cunard's famous 1936 *Queen Mary*. Ninety-six feet long and 70 feet wide, this was golden in tones and featured this electric fireplace at one end, with above a carved gesso panel *Unicorns in Battle* by Alfred J.Oakley and Gilbert Bayes. At the other end of the room was a fully equipped stage that incorporated a cinema screen with the latest sound equipment (there was a cinema room behind the gesso panel here, in which doors opened to reveal the projector). The centre of the room's floor was oak parquet, for dancing.

ABOVE LEFT AND FACING North German Lloyd's 1929 *Bremen* and 1930 *Europa* were modern transatlantic liners, and took care of their passengers' every need on that highly competitive route. These elegant items of publicity reflect its studied promotion of 'the new Tourist Class' crossing as an experience to be enjoyed in style – and also recorded.

ABOVE The Furness Withy *Queen of Bermuda* (1933) sailed between New York and Hamilton, Bermuda, but also cruised to the Caribbean. She and sister ship, *Monarch of Bermuda* – 'a sovereign ship, luxurious as the palaces which were the divine right of kings' – were two-class vessels fitted out to a high standard, and also carried some cargo. On such ships, along with those of the Grace and Matson lines, many Americans gained experience of quality leisure travel by sea. In this picture, passengers return to her by shore-based tender.

FACING Entertainment at sea was once rather more homespun than it is today – but also more genuinely communal. Passengers were content to entertain themselves rather than expecting a varied range of sophisticated facilities. Numbers on each ship were also smaller, and areas of deck space were left undesignated for improvised games such as this one.

decline), whereas *Orion* was a mid-sized, tourist-orientated liner for colonial service. Most importantly, Anderson's patronage gave O'Rorke a freedom that the corporate – indeed national – funding and planning of the transatlantic liner, with its high public profile, simply could not countenance.

The privileged enjoyed luxurious ocean travel throughout the Depression of the early 1930s, a period now cast as the 'golden age' of cruising. Existing liners were converted, and new ones built with cruising in mind – the British *Vandyck*, *Voltaire* and *Arandora Star* being examples of the former, and the Swedish *Kungsholm* best exemplifying the latter. Such ships, together with P&O's new sister ships *Strathmore*, *Strathaird* and *Stratheden* of 1932–37, helped create those timeless images of a white liner, majestically at anchor in a turquoise bay and elegantly framed with white sand and palm fronds. It is an image cruise companies still evoke today in selling the sea to a more popular market.

Certainly pictures of the lavish interiors of such period vessels, of their exotic destinations (and sometimes equally exotic passengers), offer a more attractive version of the 1930s than do photographs of the widespread poverty and deprivation. However, the Depression did have its impact on cruising: once-glamorous floating palaces from the Edwardian era, such as Cunard's *Berengaria* and White Star's *Olympic*, made brief Prohibition-busting 'booze cruises' from New York to beyond the state limit, serving up cheap gin to eager passengers at bargain prices. Cruising of sorts therefore first reached the popular market during this bizarre interlude, but economic recovery – and the Second World War – meant it would be decades before it returned. Meanwhile, shipping companies' profits from cruising were further boosted, then as now, by the low wages of most crew members – for whom, of course, the ship was for considerable periods also their home.

Getting there is half the fun!

See your Cunard-authorized Travel Agent and... GO CUNARD

QUEEN ELIZABETH · QUEEN MARY · MAURETANIA · CARONIA · BRITANNIC · MEDIA · PARTHIA · SAXONIA · FRANCONIA · SCYTHIA · SAMARIA · ASCANIA

An 18" x 22" color reproduction of this painting of the Queen Elizabeth and Queen Mary, by far the world's largest superliners (without the advertising text and suitable for framing) will be sent upon request. Write: Cunard Line, 25 Broadway, New York 4, N.Y.

During wartime, thousands of troops experienced spartan ocean travel on liners stripped of their fittings to enable them to shift whole divisions at a time. Perhaps nostalgia for such impressive ships as the *Queen Mary* did encourage some of those who underwent such bleak voyages to cruise more enjoyably on the same vessels when they were refitted after the war. However, many liners were sunk, and in the post-war years passenger fleets urgently needed rebuilding both to earn currency and to transport migrants. Britain was under additional pressure to repay war loans to the United States, and Cunard's first purpose-built cruise ship, the largely first-class *Caronia* of 1948, was primarily a dollar earner. With hull and topsides painted in three shades of green to avoid dazzle in tropical sunlight, she boasted the largest funnel afloat, proudly painted in Cunard vermillion and black; just as important, she was largely air-conditioned, and every stateroom had an en-suite bathroom. Yet handsome and luxurious though she was, *Caronia* exemplified a problem characteristic of this era of cruising: her long and costly worldwide itineraries appealed to dowager duchesses and old money, rather than to the rapidly growing middle class. In *The Cruise Ships* (1988), American maritime historian William H. Miller quotes the recollections of a former master of the vessel, and others:

> Most of the guests travelled for travel's sake, in fact there were very few places that they had not already been. The *Caronia* was a safe and familiar refuge where they could rest, be pampered and be entertained. These passengers, often of the millionaire class, often gave large and lavish parties on board, frequently for as many as 300 of their fellow voyagers.

ABOVE Stately sisters: the *Queen Elizabeth* (foreground) passes her elder sibling, *Queen Mary,* in mid Atlantic. Such a voyage seems an irresistible temptation – at least on days such as the one shown – but the aerial perspective here presages an airborne future for transatlantic passengers.

FACING TOP This captain's cocktail party would today be held inside. This photograph is aboard Orient Line's 1951 *Oronsay*, and a combination of climate and lack of air-conditioning probably made the open deck the only possible location, despite limited space. Passengers today would certainly expect a more decorative ceiling for such a formal occasion.

FACING BELOW The 'Cunard funnel' was famous, and this luggage ticket exploits it to good effect. So attached was Cunard to its funnel that, when working on the 1969 *QE2*, architect James Gardner had problems gaining approval for her black-and-white funnel design (it was later painted red andblack). The reverse of this ticket states: 'All baggage should bear one of the Company's labels showing the initial of your surname. Labels will be supplied on application to the Company's Offices.'

It seems that an American woman, one Clara Macbeth, lived for fourteen and a half years on the *Caronia* – only to be ruined by her eventual bill for US $2.5 million. Rather than addressing the future, Cunard's new ship thus embodied many of the priorities of the past. From the 1960s, jet travel seriously affected the profitability even of liners built since the Second World War, and this resulted in more of them being sent cruising. By the early 1960s, Cunard was operating four 'Green Goddesses', including the *Caronia*, having converted the transatlantic liners *Mauretania*, *Franconia* and *Carmania*. Even its flagship interwar Atlantic greyhounds, *Queen Mary* and *Queen Elizabeth*, were modified for occasional cruise voyages, but they were too big for many cruise ports, and also lacked effective air-conditioning.

Information on Harrison Line steamers from London 'to the West Indies and British Guiana' in 1930 mentioned 'lighting and ventilation ... specially fitted for tropical travelling [with] an electric fan in every state room', while Orient Line proudly advertised its 1925 liner *Otranto*, 'specifically designed for service in the tropics' on the basis of 'over forty years' experience of cruising', as boasting 'a porthole or window' in each cabin. Among the first fully air-conditioned liners were those of American Export Lines in the late 1940s, but the 1958 British passenger-cargo liner RMS *Pendennis Castle* (built specifically for the United Kingdom to Cape Town run) had air-conditioning only in first class. Britain's first fully air-conditioned liner was the 1956 *Empress of Britain* – which became the *Carnivale* some twenty years later – but decks of many British passenger vessels remained cluttered with natural draft ventilators and air intakes long after. Cruising on such ships, elegant though they might be to look at, was definitely an 'un-cool' experience – and the important American market avoided them. Today, complete air-conditioning and ship stabilizers, together with shore-based and

FACING *Canberra*'s engines-aft layout and twin funnels owed much to British tanker designs of the 1950s. Naval architect John West had designed these ships for a subsidiary of P&O, and brought this experience to the *Canberra*. The interior design of this innovative ship was overseen by the architect Sir Hugh Casson.

ABOVE 'Isn't she lovely?' This Grace Lines 1953 cruise leaflet featured their three sister ships *Santa Rosa*, *Santa Paula* and *Santa Elena*, and cleverly made the ship itself the view most to be admired.

BELOW An adjustable lamp for in-bed reading proclaims *Canberra* to be 'The First Resort', a witty gesture towards the near future in which the cruise ship would indeed become a destination in itself. But how many people now read in bed on a cruise?

"ANDES"
SUNSHINE CRUISES - 1959
ROYAL MAIL LINES

ABOVE Sunshine and style are here on offer aboard Royal Mail Lines' luxurious 1939 *Andes*. Artistic licence has greatly enhanced the dimensions of the swimming pool but – as ever – the social (and feminine) appeal of the pool outweighs any 'romance of the ocean', which is here carefully designed out by depiction of the ship's appealing terraces and pool-side umbrellas.

FACING Period decor and dresses – and smiles all round – here aboard Cunard's 1955 *Ivernia*. Launched for the transatlantic route from Liverpool to Canada and New York, she was soon turned to cruising. In 1963 she emerged from extensive refitting as the green-painted *Franconia*, complete with pools, air-conditioning, and state rooms offering private facilities. Sold, she became the Russian *Fedor Shalyapin* in 1973.

onboard information systems that allow ships to avoid really severe weather, make for cooler and calmer passenger conditions.

The success of cruising as we know it today lies in purpose-built new tonnage, but in Britain at least certain ships acquired a regular clientele who returned to travel on them year after year. In the late 1990s, attempts were made by those passengers loyal to P&O's 1961 *Canberra* to save the elderly vessel from being broken up (though how she could have been used, or even maintained, was unclear). Such quasi-tribal affections were rooted in the ways certain groups within British society adopted particular ships as especially appropriate to their lifestyles and outlook. The elegant Royal Mail Lines' *Andes* (launched in 1939, but on war service until 1948) was designed for style, and carried only first- and second-class passengers. A 1959 brochure for her 'Sunshine Cruises' stressed: 'Attractive as ports of call may be, it is upon the ship that depends the real enjoyment.' It went on to celebrate the ship's virtues: 'Luxurious decor, cuisine for the epicure and superb service ... dining saloons in which all passengers can be accommodated at one time.'

From 1960 *Andes* was converted to cruising, and a crew member quoted by Miller recalls that, in the latter years of that decade, sailing on her from Southampton 'was like the first day back at school', since almost all the passengers knew one another; she was 'an exceptionally elegant ship, much like a floating clubhouse'. *Andes* was scrapped in 1971, but her last years must have sorely tried the loyalty even of her determined regulars: 'Pipes were bursting, the air-conditioning would break down and there would be plumbing problems. But most of the passengers were deep loyalists and accepted these problems and discomforts.'

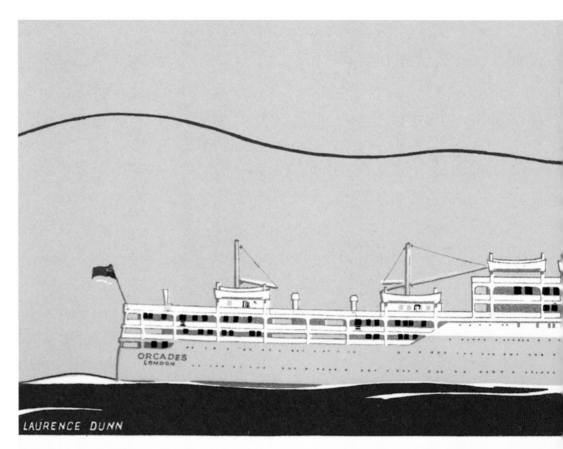

THE NEW ORIE

ABOVE A stylized publicity profile by Laurence Dunn of Orient Line's 1937 *Orcades*; Dunn was also responsible for choosing the attractive corn hull colour. *Orcades'* maiden cruise was to the Mediterranean, departing Southampton on 21 August that year.

ABOVE Souvenir pennants such as this, from one of *Uganda's* many educational voyages, no doubt once hung alongside other mementoes in children's bedrooms across Britain – just as they were designed to do.

FACING This pocket-sized souvenir lifebuoy from P&O's 1950 *Chusan* combines an immediate nautical appeal with suitably informative lettering. Real lifebuoys carry only the name of the vessel and its port of registry.

Well-defined loyalties to certain ships extended also to the competition *Andes* faced: the tourist-class *Reina del Mar*, launched in 1956 as a liner for the Liverpool to South America run, but operating as a cruise ship from the early 1960s, catered, according to Miller's interviewee, 'to corporate Britain, [while] the *Andes* carried aristocratic Britain'. Whether strictly true or not, it seems that (then as now) certain companies and vessels acquired reputations – and associations – just as fixed as those of any land resort.

In the 1960s, British vessels from the P&O, Orient Line, Union-Castle and Shaw Savill fleets all offered good-value voyages from Southampton to the Mediterranean consciously aimed at a newly affluent home market. This was a real glimpse of the future and despite sailing sunward on hastily purchased folding aluminium garden chairs amid forests of largely redundant cargo gear, these representatives of middle England must indeed have felt that, in Prime Minister Harold MacMillan's immortal phrase, they had 'never had it so good'. A 1960 P&O advertisement perhaps caught the spirit of the time better than intended: 'More and more busy people are realizing the tremendous value of the restored health, time for thought, and new business associates that only sea travel can give. ... Don't forget to bring your wife!'

Union Castle promoted its *Transvaal Castle* as a 'Floating Hotel, South Atlantic ... fully air-conditioned', and stressed that there were no 'class' barriers: '*Every* passenger has the freedom of her broad decks, her sun-soaked pool, her big cinema, her dining room, lounges, bars and playrooms.' These were good times, but they were not to last. A decade later nearly all of these British liners that had introduced sedate cruising to the middle class were hit by the oil crisis that followed the Six Day War of 1967, by the decline of the British economy, and by severe government restrictions on foreign

INER, R.M.S. "ORCADES", 23,000 TONS.

exchange. Hitherto popular and successful ships such as *Chusan, Himalaya, Orcades, Oronsay, Orsova, Reina Del Mar, Northern Star* and *Ocean Monarch* all made their final voyages to Taiwanese ship breakers.

The 'educational cruises' operated by vessels of the British India Steam Navigation Company were an unusual feature of the British cruising scene during the 1960s and 1970s. The company had also operated troop ships and passenger vessels serving British colonies, and four of these, *Devonia, Dunera, Nevasa,* and *Uganda,* were converted to take schoolchildren on educational trips lasting some two weeks in European waters. Best-known was the SS *Uganda,* built in 1952 and converted in 1966–67 to an educational cruise ship for 920 children, but with a completely segregated area for 306 adult passengers. *Uganda* had operated with *Kenya* on the colonial East Africa run, and her adult passenger section was, from 1967, possibly the last example of a somewhat eccentric seagoing regime that nevertheless befitted the grand name of her owner (and, no doubt, the outlook of her passengers). Memories of the former cruise director on board *Uganda,* Alan Wells – whose duties also included entertainment – are recorded by Miller:

> The elevator operator ... was a bearded Indian, straight out of the Imperial Raj, who wore white gloves ... Evenings included frog racing and a ship's concert [featuring the] singing surgeon, the plumber-magician, the chief engineer who did a monologue, the engineers who staged a *corps de ballet* and all of this emceed by the deputy captain. There was ... an Indian band, always a quartet, that played before lunch just like in some grand seaside hotel.

The many faces of the great sea holiday.

The Smoking Room on *Uganda* was 'complete with leather chairs and mounted elephant tusks ... like a gentleman's club from the last century. Nothing ever happened here – just chats and drinks'. Many passengers, it would seem, blended in all too well with such decor: 'They were mostly retired professionals and consequently the age range was rather high. There were virtually never any children travelling in the adult quarters ... We also had lots of retired military.' These passengers 'always helped decorate the lounge before a party or special occasion. They were a well-travelled group, the type of passengers who liked lots of non-fiction in the library'.

The school cruises on *Uganda* were an enlightened concept, and are remembered with affection by many: a friend recalls that her own two-week cruise had the ambitious aim of visiting five of the seven 'Ancient Wonders of the World'. *Uganda* served as a hospital ship in the Falklands War, and when she was eventually laid up, a committee was formed to save Britain's 'last colonial liner' – but she went for scrap in 1986.

It is hard now to accept that *Uganda*'s colonial-style cruises virtually overlapped with the 249 one-hour voyages of the 'Love Boat' on American television beginning in 1977. This popular series was partly set aboard the *Pacific Princess* (initially it was set on the *Sun Princess*), operated by P&O's successful American subsidiary, Princess Cruises, based in Los Angeles. Unusually, the Princess fleet comprised sleek, purpose-built vessels with state-of-the-art design and fashionable 'mod' interiors that made ideal locations for escapist television. With its compelling setting featuring white liners, palm fronds and limpid turquoise water, and storylines that highlighted romance, camaraderie and hospitality, the TV show was a hit. The series is credited with helping to popularize cruising in the United States, with almost 20 percent of the ship's passengers reportedly booking after seeing the show.

Ships to have and to hold: these two images capture the special affection that ships evoke.

FACING An information officer for Chandris Lines cradles a model of *Ellinis* (built in 1932 at Quincy, Massachusetts, as the *Lurline* for Matson Lines), which was purchased in 1963. First operated by Chandris on the Britain–Australia emigrant run, *Ellenis* later cruised with 1,642 tourist berths, but was laid up in 1980.

ABOVE A model of Cunard's *Queen Mary*, a vessel now preserved at Long Beach, California, by the British manufacturer Dinky Toys. Their popular items reflected the post-war transport world. This six-and-a-half-inch (16.5 cm) model has seen better days, and tells its own story of the passing of such classic ocean liners.

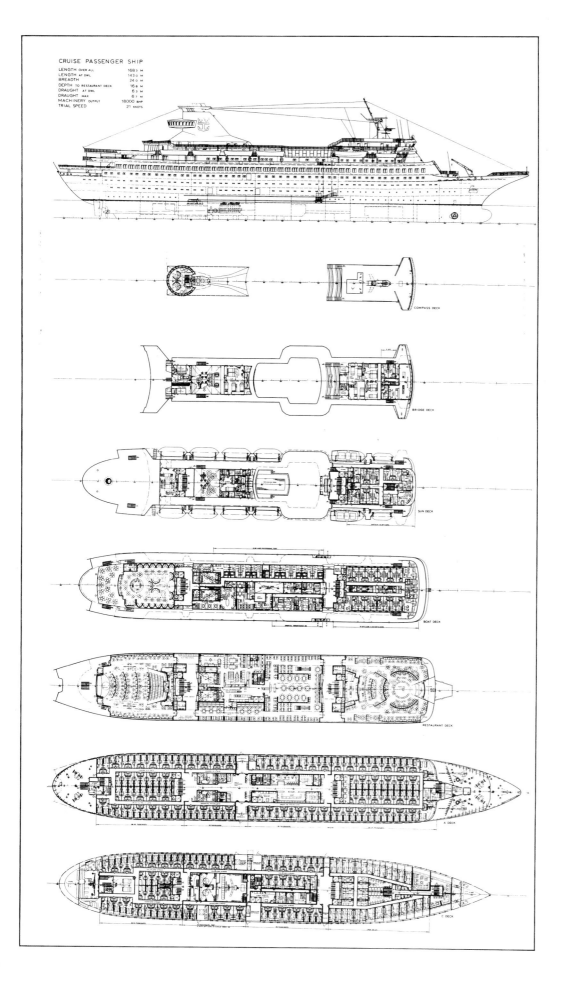

CRUISE PASSENGER SHIP

LENGTH OVER ALL	168·3 M
LENGTH AT DWL	143·0 M
BREADTH	24·0 M
DEPTH TO RESTAURANT DECK	16·8 M
DRAUGHT AT DWL	6·3 M
DRAUGHT MAX	6·7 M
MACHINERY OUTPUT	18000 BHP
TRIAL SPEED	21 KNOTS

COMPASS DECK

BRIDGE DECK

SUN DECK

BOAT DECK

RESTAURANT DECK

A DECK

DECK

Welcome aboard

From the moment you walk up the gangway to be met by a welcome smile from a steward, the great life aboard Britanis starts to happen. From now on all the many advantages of travelling by sea begin to unfold.

Like every other fully air-conditioned ocean-going ship of Chandris Lines, Britanis offers the one really comfortable, relaxed and civilised way of getting from one part of the world to another. It's sunshine and fresh air all the way, while stopping off at fascinating ports of call adds to the pleasure of your voyage. And with all those leisurely entertainments and facilities provided for your pleasure at no extra cost – there's no better way to cross the globe.

Sea travel also gives you the much needed opportunity to prepare and acclimatise yourself before setting foot in a new continent. There are no sudden time differentials to upset your equilibrium. No sudden jumping from one extreme of temperature to another. And you may take all the baggage you need . . . and it travels along with you.

So, wherever you'd going – have a glorious long relaxing time getting there aboard Britanis. Britanis . . . where getting from A to B probably means no more than taking the lift from the Beauty Salon to the Waikiki Dining Room !

Now let the steward take your luggage and escort you to the comfortably appointed accommodation reserved for you.

From the 1960s onwards in New York, meanwhile, the ocean-liner piers of Manhattan welcomed a succession of liners whose design, in differing ways, reflected the new importance of cruising. Exceptions were the new Italian liners *Leonardo Da Vinci*, *Michelangelo* and *Raffaello*, and the Gallic 'ship of state', *France*. These were vessels designed only with prestigious Atlantic service in mind, and lavishly subsidized accordingly by their respective governments. Their pampered careers ended in the mid-1970s: *France* later underwent radical transformation to become the successful cruise ship *Norway*, but it was not economic to convert the Italian vessels. Scrapped long before their time, their fate brutally demonstrated that in the new jet age, passenger ships had to cruise to keep afloat.

The interiors on Holland America's 1959 *Rotterdam*, the first of the new armada to emerge from under New York's Verrazano Narrows Suspension Bridge, were divided into first and tourist class through horizontal layering, rather than by vertical subdivisions, an arrangement that gave passengers access to entire decks of accommodation. A back-to-back staircase amidships accessed all decks, but partitions could be closed on alternate decks to give a seamless two-class system for transatlantic voyages; with partitions retracted, the ship became a one-class cruise ship. The regular New York vessels still attracted a far more discerning clientele than their counterparts sailing from Miami and Fort Lauderdale – ships that served predominantly the new cruise market from increasingly popular Florida ports. Modern liners sailing in the 1960s from the famous piers of mid-town Manhattan were among the finest and most technically sophisticated ever built – and certainly the most expensive.

Rotterdam herself was as innovative in profile as in layout. Although placing machinery spaces aft was not revolutionary (Matson Line had done this with its *Lurline* in 1908), it did allow a spacious top sun-deck where most earlier ships had cluttering funnels and ventilators, and this greatly enhanced

ABOVE Illustration from a 1971 Chandris Lines booklet: 'From the moment you walk up the gangway to be met by a welcome smile from a steward, the great life aboard *Britanis* starts to happen.' Stewards here line up to greet passengers aboard, and to carry their luggage. Today baggage is loaded (and security screened) separately, and then brought direct to passengers' cabins but that initial greeting remains as important as ever.

FACING This detailed deck plan from a company publication for the 1971 *Nordic Prince* (one of three sisters completed between 1970 and 1972) illustrates the ship's distinctive profile and funnel-mounted Viking Crown Lounge. The bow-mounted transverse propeller, for unassisted manoeuvring in port, can also be seen. Cutaway profiles of vessels have long been used in promotional material, but this is almost a scaled-down reproduction of plans drawn for the construction of the ship. Its clarity and professionalism have a special appeal.

ABOVE The indoor pool on the 1959 *Rotterdam*. In keeping with the careful use of artworks throughout the vessel, the wall decorations here are sculptures by the Delft artist Jan Rot, and – given the location – are sensibly constructed of aluminium.

LEFT The La Venezia icecream bar was located forward on the 1959 *Rotterdam*'s promenade deck. Modern cruise ships have taken to new heights the recreation of fashionable locales (often from Italy) as venues for socializing, as here, and for onboard shopping.

FACING Pool-side life, Italian style, on the sundeck of Costa Line's 1958 *Federico C.*, as presented in a 1978 brochure. The company's flagship when built, she originally carried 1,279 passengers in three classes, but in 1970 turned to one-class cruising with 800 berths. She had 'seven bars, four lido swimming pools, quality orchestras, and radio-telephone communication'.

ABOVE A brochure for German Atlantic Line's 1969 *Hamburg* tried hard, but not entirely successfully, for the personal touch: 'You'll always find me near the swimming pool and Lido Bar. I'm Wilhelm Hink, the deck steward. And I'm partial to sunners and sportsmen.'

LEFT A ship is first and foremost technology that moves, and promotional material often emphasizes the latest developments. Here, a careful mix of soft-focus flowers, fresh fruit, white telephones – and omnipresent TV sets – sets the style for boldly going on *Hamburg*, billed as the 'space ship'.

FACING Publicity for the 1965 *Oceanic* adopted a futuristic magradome-style page layout to highlight this feature of the ship's many amenities, itself typical of *Oceanic*'s imaginative and practical design: retractable glazed sliding roof sections allowed use of the vessel's pool and lido area in all weathers, and these became a standard feature on cruise ships.

MAGRODOME OPENED

MAGRODOME CLOSED

§OCEANIC

SO UNIQUE!
THE ALL-WEATHER MAGIC
OF THE MAGRODOME

The Lido Deck on the OCEANIC is an indoor deck .... and an outdoor deck, thanks to the retractable Magrodome roof! It slides open or closed, depending on the weather, allowing you to swim and play from first day to last.

At night, it's transformed into a colorful setting for promenading, toasting new-found friends or for a final dip in one of 2 pools. Popular deck sports and games keep the daytime fun going... with sauna, massage rooms and a modern gymnasium to help keep you in shape.

her passenger facilities. Good design was well-repaid, and *Rotterdam* proved an enduringly successful vessel; her distinctive ambience made her a luxurious 'home from home' for countless loyal passengers over four decades of service. Decoratively, she was a showcase of outstanding Dutch contemporary design, featuring exotic veneers and abstract Delft bas reliefs. Opulent and alluring, she also possessed the most wonderful aromas of expensive cigars, French polish, perfume, leather and (as a turbine ship) steam. *Rotterdam* enchanted all her passengers, and exemplified modern luxury on the high seas. In 1969, she was refitted as a cruise ship, and never again visited her namesake home port under the Holland America flag; the line itself eventually relocated to Seattle for commercial reasons.

The elegant and luxurious 1966 Swedish motor liner *Kungsholm* also catered specifically to New York's wealthy cruise fraternity. Her engine space was two-thirds aft, but her two funnels (the forward one a dummy) gave a traditional and balanced silhouette; in Manhattan such functionality of proportions (rather than mere engineering) mattered. Between the funnels was an innovative terraced lido complex, with shelter screens and 'wings' projecting between the lifeboats amidships to give a multi-layered outdoor environment. This offered quiet corners for relaxing with a good book, while Swedish American Line's impeccably trained deck stewards in immaculate uniforms brought blankets, drinks and snacks. Again, the ambience on this vessel differed from that on the cruise ships sailing from Florida: aboard *Kungsholm* a quiet emphasis on being at sea was the keynote, rather than any obligation to 'entertain' constantly.

West Germany's 1969 *Hamburg* had similar deck arrangements to the *Kungsholm* – but a quite remarkable funnel in the form of a slender cone sprouting angled stovepipes topped with a giant flying saucer. Her interiors were by Munich-based architect Georg Manner, whose approach resembled that of

ABOVE Sculpted deck terraces at the stern of Star Cruises' 1995 *Superstar Gemini* (built 1992 as *Crown Jewel*), complete with potted plants, form the venue for a barbecue. A great deal of attention is now paid, as here, to ensuring that suitable lighting is installed to make such areas attractive after dark as well.

FACING P&O's 1953 liner *Arcadia* reappears at an African port. This photograph illustrates the frequent separateness of a cruise ship, in style and technology, from its ever-changing surroundings.

Mies van der Rohe; rich palisander veneers, marble and leather-upholstered modernist furniture produced a unique minimalist aesthetic that was distinctly Teutonic. Certainly, it was the obverse of the German baroque found on her Edwardian predecessors. The *Hamburg* was one of two stylish and innovative vessels backed by the New York-based Dane Axel Bitsch-Christiensen, a dynamic figure in the city's travel trade in the 1960s. The other was the 1965 *Oceanic*, Italian-designed and built for Home Lines, which was an interesting consortium of Italian, Greek and Swedish interests. Of the liners sailing regularly from New York, the *Oceanic* was easily the most advanced, and the design approach of her international owners can now be seen as pre-figuring a shift in the cruise industry from nationalism as a selling point to more flexible and imaginative representations of leisure and entertainment at sea.

In retrospect, it is ironic that many New York cruise aficionados looked down on the new party-orientated fleets sailing from Florida, since these had the initiative in cruising and flourished as a result. Home Lines, Swedish American and German Atlantic Line all closed operations in the 1970s and 1980s, while Carnival, Royal Caribbean and NCL have come to dominate the industry, at least in the northern hemisphere. NCL's parent company is Malaysian-owned Star Cruises, a comparatively recent but fast-growing company that terms itself 'The World's Only Global Cruise Line' – though a similar claim is also made by Carnival.

The unchanging romance of a cruise still offers the best of terrestrial and oceanic worlds: a comfortable sea-view apartment at an ever-changing, but always desirable, address. A 1935 P&O advertisement for round-the-world voyages captured just these attractions: 'From start to finish of the voyage you will live in the same ship, with service and accommodation at least equalling those of a

ABOVE This steward, seated on his bed in a tiny cabin, is immaculately turned out, with personal possessions neatly arranged: a Phillips radio and an Indian calendar showing a bullock cart and Triumph Herald saloon car on a rural road. It is March 1965, aboard P&O's *Canberra*. Souvenir lifebuoys from the liners *Strathmore* and *Orsova* (probably previous postings) hang on the walls, while on the desk lies a 'Cold Weather Clothing Issue Card', and the shelves hold (along with spare Osram light bulbs for passengers' cabins) paperback fiction including Neville Shute, John Creasey, Ngaio Marsh and Mary Stewart. Apart from the photograph (of his wife?), the telephone is the most important object here.

ABOVE RIGHT P&O officers line up on foredeck of the *Oronsay* in immaculate whites to practise their drills. The long shadows here suggest early morning, while most passengers would still be safely asleep. The crew's seemingly effortless smart presentation later in the day will be the result of this early practice.

FACING A small group of P&O officers practise their saluting skills in the ship's games room. Decorative letters on the floor suggest that this is Orient Line's 1954 *Orsova*.

FACING BELOW Meeting the captain and officers for cocktails is an occasion much appreciated by passengers as a unique opportunity to ask questions (though to the other side they must become all too predictable). At this party aboard P&O's *Oronsay*, deck ratings are also present, probably in a serving capacity.

luxury hotel, and you will have, besides, the many attractions of life at sea and pleasant interludes at the various ports of call.' Five years earlier, the English writer Evelyn Waugh had taken a similar line in the fashionable magazine *Harper's Bazaar*, describing cruising as 'a pursuit entirely of its own kind ... not a bogus kind of travelling, but an entirely new sport, with its own aims and rules'. One should voyage, he felt, 'primarily for rest and change of scene and comfort', and wickedly suggested that recreation was to be found not in 'the study of foreign places and people' but rather in 'the study of one's fellow-passengers among foreign places'.

Sea travel in the early decades of the twentieth century offered far more choice of routes than today. Countless ships served hundreds of ports worldwide on a regular basis. Many cargo vessels also carried some passengers, who could plan their own voyage on the basis of a vessel's route, size, nationality and cost. For those with individual cabins, such a mode of travel offered valued peace and quiet, and Waugh found this most congenial and (at least compared with hotels he frequented ashore) very economical. Sea voyaging, as he knew it, survives now only in some aspects of freighter travel, and at the luxury end of the cruise market. 'The qualities which struck me most,' he recalled, 'were its outstanding comfort and leisure', noting that 'the ship's business is to carry you where you want to go and to make you as comfortable as they can on the journey'. Waugh also touched on the recurrent appeal of the 'nautical style' for architects in finding 'an integrity and decency about a ship which one rarely finds on land except in very old-fashioned and expensive hotels'. Integrity or not, though, freedom was the most powerful appeal of cruising, and *Vogue* expressed this succinctly in 1936 in observing: 'The least that a ship does is to take you to places. The most it does is to free you.'

Yet the self-contained, hotel-like nature of a ship that Waugh identified differentiates it from all other forms of travel, and does remain intrinsic to its fascination. In fact, a cruise ship can be said to comprise at least three distinct worlds: that of its carefree passengers, that of the officers, and that of a crew drawn today from more than fifty different countries – though officers and senior engineers are mostly white male Europeans. These different onboard worlds rarely overlap (though a service door left open may give a passenger a glimpse of a more spartan world), but their faultless interlocking is essential if the ship is to function properly. Any malfunction here can be quite startling. The American author Peter Kohler recalls a 1970s incident in which two of *QE2*'s Scottish engineers, sweating heartily and swearing heavily in best Glaswegian, emerged from a service door into a first-class corridor sporting the time-honoured gear of boiler suits unbuttoned to the waist – to the considerable consternation of passengers dressed in full evening attire.

Some vessels, such as Cunard's *QM2*, still offer distinct facilities for different categories of passenger, while the life of senior officers bears little similarity to that of cabin and cleaning staff. Officers will have well-appointed cabins and mess rooms (companies must provide these to attract and retain good people), while more lowly staff may share fairly cramped bunk accommodation. Here, too, a cruise ship mirrors employment patterns found through the developed world, though unions agree that most cruise companies now provide fair wages and acceptable conditions. Internationality is one trait of this floating world, for a cruise ship may be designed, built, owned, crewed and registered in five or more different countries. Onboard style and cuisine is usually cosmopolitan chic, with restaurants and shopping arcades often named after those in noted tourist cities.

ABOVE Pleasure Island. This view of the liner *Disney Magic* moored alongside at Castaway Cay, Disney's private island, shows how the island docking arrangement ensures easy access to shore facilities for passengers; this was a key consideration for Disney in constructing this expensive guest facility. At other cruise company beach resorts in the Caribbean and Bahamas, passengers usually have to disembark into tenders in order to be taken ashore. Here, ship and shore are securely united as part of one vacation experience.

FACING The cruise liners *Disney Magic* and *Disney Wonder* were conceived and designed to be different from other cruise ships in appearance, and in interior decor. Externally, they feature elements drawn from a wide era of passenger travel by sea, from sailing ship era gilded bow decoration to twin funnels (the forward one is an observation lounge) and hull colours from the classic transatlantic liner era. The Disney Cruise Terminal at Port Canaveral, seen here, is itself styled with a nod to Southampton's now-vanished transatlantic passenger terminal; it was specially constructed at the same time as the two ships it would serve.

In their marketing, cruise companies understandably cultivate a carefree image, but in reality their activities are by no means divorced from political issues. A winter 1929–30 brochure from the American Clyde-Malloy shipping company advertised its steamers *Evangeline* and *Iroquois* as 'affording every comfort of modern ocean travel [in] direct DAILY overnight service in each direction between these famous resort centers of Florida and Cuba'. By autumn 1937 the company was operating another three ships to 'the cool Atlantic, Miami and Havana, St Augustine ... Texas and other Resorts', while shifts in language and culture make wonderfully appropriate its claim that 'more and more people are discovering the glorious possibilities of a summer vacation in gay Miami Beach'. When Carnival purchased the Italian company Costa Cruises in 1998, its cruises from the Mediterranean to Cuba ceased in compliance with the US Government embargo, and today no ships offer an 'overnight service' between Miami and Havana – though they may well do so post-Castro. Since 9/11, security has been increased, with electronic passenger smart cards linked to visual scanning, ships escorted in and out of port, and underwater checks on vessels in port by divers. Companies also employ other unspecified measures but, given developments in aircraft security, at least some cruise 'guests' are probably wide awake – and armed.

The cruise industry in Florida has flourished by identifying and exploiting new possibilities, but nostalgia is also a crucial element here. Even the sinking of the White Star liner *Titanic* on her maiden voyage in 1912 is now recycled as part of this 'romance'; passengers (and crew) can be photographed against a backdrop of the grand staircase featured in James Cameron's 1997 film – which, to the great relief of the cruise industry, proved a boost to business. The *Titanic* was a transatlantic liner; but cruising has eagerly assumed the mantle of such historic vessels as the *Ile de France, Normandie, Queen*

Mary and *Queen Elizabeth*, or *Rex*, with some cruise ships sporting rooms directly inspired by them, or displaying period memorabilia. The design and promotion of Cunard's *Queen Mary 2* from the start stressed her place in tradition, with emphasis on retro design and period style, both inside and out. Her funnel deliberately echoes the more elegant (and aerodynamically functional) structure designed by architect James Gardner for the 1969 *QE2*, while on board a permanent Heritage Trail exhibition features Cunard passengers since the 1840s.

In these aspects of their entertainment provision cruise ships parallel leisure developments ashore: a steel and concrete life-size replica of the *Titanic* is being constructed in a Shanghai shopping centre (with other world architectural icons planned). In her wide-ranging study of contemporary leisure and entertainment culture, *Fun! Leisure and Landscape*, Tracy Metz has noted the breaking of the 'traditional link between place and function' as typical of recent leisure sites, and cites the equally bizarre examples of the climbing wall on new Royal Caribbean cruise ships and Monte Cervino, an artificial crag in a Rotterdam outdoor sports centre, whose outer and, if it rains, inner surfaces can be climbed. In more ways than one, perhaps, leisure culture is all at sea.

To cruise is to buy, however unconsciously, into the romantic mythology of seafaring. Each ship tends to have its own personality. This reflects the priorities of those who commission and design it, shaped in turn partly by passengers themselves, who bring to a cruise their own expectations of adventure and entertainment afloat. Disney entered the cruise market in 1998 with its first ship, *Disney Magic*; its second, *Disney Wonder*, followed a year later. The two ships were built simultaneously in Italy and a retro-style passenger terminal was dedicated to Disney at Port Canaveral. Disney also understood well the need to create a specific entertainment environment,

ABOVE *Dreamward* undergoes major surgery at Lloyd Werft's shipyard in Bremerhaven, Germany in 1998 to become the *Norwegian Dream*. Cruise ships, like cargo vessels, are sometimes enlarged ('jumboized') by being cut in two to allow the insertion of a preconstructed centre section. Computer-aided design allows modern vessels to be designed with this possibility in mind.

FACING ABOVE A photograph of the Viscountess D'Orthez aboard Cunard's *QE2*. The image powerfully reinforces the appeal of that special maritime domesticity, a seagoing 'home from home', that remains a powerful appeal of cruising. Today, TV is standard in all cabins, rather than a luxury to be so proudly displayed.

FACING BELOW The *QE2* on trials in late 1968, during which she achieved 32.46 knots. She has her original charcoal-and-white funnel, later repainted in Cunard's traditional red and black.

and paid great attention to the design and ambience of the embarkation terminal: the cruise's special magic had to begin there. It complemented this with the acquisition of 'Castaway Cay', an island in the Bahamas that it purchased outright. As Disney itself expressed it: 'An industry first, the island was designed with its own dock, providing guests the ability to walk ashore.' The company placed great importance on passengers being able to walk ashore directly from the ship, and have deliberately only developed part of the island.

Both the Disney ships themselves and the Port Canaveral cruise terminal were designed with detailed input from Walt Disney Imagineering to ensure that they enhanced customer choice within the wide range of entertainment already offered by the company at its successful land resorts: Disney Cruise Line offered guests 'an exciting new way to vacation with Disney'. In this sense, it was an important part of the new ships' role to extend seaward the distinctive Disney-brand vacation and leisure experience. The exact balance between the increasingly self-contained experience offered by large modern cruise ships and shore visits – sometimes to Caribbean islands owned or leased by individual cruise companies – can be fraught. The ships of Royal Caribbean carry on their sides the slogan 'like no holiday on earth', but writing in Britain's *Daily Telegraph* in November 1999, travel correspondent Carole Cadwalladr felt that a cruise with them '*is* like a vacation on earth. It is just nothing like a vacation at sea'.

In the twenty-first century, a cruise allows passengers to experience a repackaging of that ephemeral Art Deco age when the great passenger ships of different nations battled for the honour of flying the Blue Riband for the fastest Atlantic crossing, while film stars, aristocrats and industrial magnates danced the night away on board. Back then, the first-class accommodation of prestige liners was only

for a select few, but today, broad cross-sections of society can enjoy upmarket facilities and decor. Cunard's *Queen Mary 2* boasts a full orchestra and dance floor, but most dancing is now strictly disco (which needs little space and no orchestra). In their lavish interior spaces and grand decor, cruise ships offer a five-star experience at bargain prices. Interestingly, despite their inventive decor, Carnival's designer Joe Farcus intends his ships to be 'essentially anachronistic' in the privileged experience of service and surroundings they offer passengers, and co-ordinates a range of 'luxurious' and 'exotic' features to achieve this. Although alert to the pull of nostalgia, Farcus employs designs more original than the cautious pastel shades so often found in cruise-ship interiors.

Floating culture capsules to their passengers, the impact of cruise ships and their passengers upon port communities and upon the environment itself is nevertheless hotly debated. There have been some high-profile fines for illegal release of waste, and companies are keen to publicize the technological sophistication of the systems fitted in all new vessels to reduce to an absolute minimum any pollution of sea or air. The risk of sea pollution is no small issue as a cruise ship processes up to 140,000 gallons of sewage, and up to 1.2 million gallons of grey water daily. And then there is all the garbage, which modern vessels compact, dry and incinerate. All ships designed after 2004 will incorporate Advanced Water Processing Systems (AWPS); modern diesel engines are designed to achieve virtually zero emissions, while gas turbines are even more environmentally friendly. Nevertheless, the inherently intrusive nature of large cruise ships in remote or beautiful areas (both popular destinations for cruises), and the considerable impact of their several thousand passengers when they disembark, ensure that the environmental issue will remain under close scrutiny at both the local and international level. Even small changes can make a difference for the better – and the world's first

soluble golf ball was announced in early 2005. No longer need cruise ships mark their routes with an ever-increasing seabed trail of shiny white plastic spheres.

Neither pollution nor over-fishing has lessened the essential fascination of the ocean. Equally, it retains its ability to swallow ships, though glossy cruise brochures avoid mention of that, and those companies operating 'classic' (meaning older) cruise ships rarely detail their vessels' age or safety specifications. There have been few major cruise-ship disasters (and none involving modern vessels) so, apart from some well-publicized instances of food poisoning on board ships, in general the industry deserves its air of professional yet relaxed reassurance. For Florida, the boom in cruising has spectacularly reinvented its 1920s' role as the 'sunshine state', but this time for international visitors rather than just 'snowbirds' fleeing the cold winters of New York and other northern American cities. The obvious pleasures of Florida cruising are certainly a far cry from publicity pictures of rug-wrapped passengers on the North Atlantic run 'enjoying' mugs of cocoa served by indomitable British deck stewards.

As a broader cultural phenomenon, the growing popularity of 'mass-market' cruising also reflects social trends over the last half-century. The global cruise industry relies upon a well-developed service sector and on buoyant consumerism, but the appeal is fun. Aboard a cruise ship, passengers can assume different identities and move easily between contrasting experiences secure in the knowledge that reality is hours, days or weeks away – back on land. Time assumes a different pace, and through drinking, dancing, eating, gambling and romance, multi-sensory experiences are heightened in a novel ambience whose decor and lighting encourage just such shifts.

In some ways cruise ships are indeed floating cities, but – unlike the real cities they emulate – they are highly controlled and secure environments. Their wholly enclosed and entertaining artificiality sets them apart both from the often feared public spaces to be found in their passengers' home cities, and from the potentially challenging values of their foreign destinations. Staying on board is one way to avoid any upset; another is for the cruise industry to control and commodify all environments that passengers are likely to encounter – on shore as well as at sea. The near future may offer life in a gated suburb, mall shopping on CCTV (closed circuit television) – and 'escape' vacations on a floating agglomeration of top-brand shops and fine restaurants to a sanitized 'foreign' destination featuring more top-brand shops, a purpose-built straw market, and local stalls selling T-shirts made in China. Book now to avoid disappointment.

Entertainment

Cruising today is entertainment from start to finish, from show lounge to shore visits – excerpts of which may be screened that evening on cabin TV, both to amuse those who took part and to attract any doubters next time. The ship itself is designed as an ongoing show, with each destination an interval. Between the wars, cruising reflected the very different spirit of the times in emphasizing the benefits of fresh air and the outdoor life. It was no coincidence that Hitler's *Kraft durch Freude* ('Strength through Joy') movement commissioned two large cruise ships specifically for the benefit of German workers – and to secure their votes. There was none of the vast, tinted glass screens that feature so prominently on vessels today; passengers were typically depicted leaning over the handrail and enjoying the ocean breeze, though a brochure for Orient Line's 1937 *Orcades* did specifically stress the 'protection from the wind' provided by her novel deck 'windscreens with their impressive curved hoods'. As for onboard entertainment, a policy of what might be described as polite inertia characterized the attitude of cruise companies: indoors it was drinking and smoking, dining, dancing and the ship's cinema, while on deck it was tennis, improvised party-type games and the inevitable deck quoits.

For a January 1932 cruise by Orient Line's SS *Otranto*, the brochure stressed that 'an ample supply of deck chairs' was provided for the free use of passengers, while 'Entertainments on Board' stated only: 'A Band for dancing will be carried and there will be concerts, deck sports, and other entertainments on board during the cruise.' An idea of the latter can be gleaned from the fact that the onboard shop carried 'fancy dress costumes and bathing dresses'. Such traditions died hard. On a 1951 cruise, P&O's *Chusan* advertised (via a hand-typed sheet) a 'Combined Children's Fancy Dress and Concert Party' to be held 'On the Promenade Dance Space' at 3.00pm on Sunday. Events included dances, poems, songs and games by children aged six to eleven years, and 'Musical Bumps'; music was provided by the

ABOVE Cool drink, hot pants – and a coded question. Just cut out the coupon and send off. Few advertisements today are quite so explicit – yet so coy – in suggesting what mutually rewarding interpersonal relationships might flour sh during a cruise.

FACING Deck quoits aboard P&O's 1961 *Canberra*. Modern ships offer jogging tracks and tennis, but the pressure of numbers (and changing fashions in deck games) has brought the near demise of this traditional game, which requires a fair amount of deck space for relatively few players.

ABOVE Developing sea-legs, limbo-style, and with microphone commentary from a uniformed master of ceremonies. These are improvised games aboard the 1965 *Sagafjord*, operated by Norwegian America Line (later Norwegian America Cruises). She ran Pacific summer cruises, with a once-a-year world cruise for three months each winter, and carried 789 passengers. *Sagafjord* regularly received the highest ratings from cruise professionals and, with her sister ship *Vistafjord*, was considered one of the best cruise ships afloat.

LEFT Deck games aboard Hamburg Atlantic Line's *Hanseatic* (acquired in 1959 having been built 1930 as *Empress of Scotland* and now carefully featuring her new owner's funnel logo): 'Shuffleboard you can enjoy even as a spectator. The special tourist-class sports area is also protected from the breezes which may blow from any direction. Relax! Feel yourself at home.'

FACING Expectant young faces and 'native' costumes are captured in this engagingly innocent glimpse of entertainment aboard Orient Line's 1951 *Oronsay*, en route from Australia to Britain that year. Such impromptu events were an accepted way of passing the time on long voyages.

ABOVE The ladies engage in an evening's (mechanical) horse-racing, probably aboard Orient Line's *Oronsay*. The gentleman in the background sports a black tie, and a general air of propriety reigns, notwithstanding any possible (organized) excitement.

FACING ABOVE An elegant evening of fur wraps and guitar music, with officers in attendance, around the First Class pool aboard Hamburg Atlantic's *Hanseatic* in 1959. This ship carried only 85 first-class passengers, as against 1,165 tourist-class, and the atmosphere here is of an elite both self-contained and self-assured.

FACING BELOW Repairing the effect of those sea breezes aboard the Black Sea Shipping Company's 1964 *Adjaria* – 'When on board you are certain to feel the national style at once. It is everywhere.' And domestic goddesses hard at work in a communal washing and ironing room on P&O's 1937 *Stratheden*, an unusual facility also provided over twenty years later on the company's *Canberra*.

ship's orchestra. 'Entertainments' aboard the *Andes* in 1959 (of which a programme was published daily) included 'Deck Quoits, Deck Tennis, Shuffleboard and other deck games, together with Table Tennis', while 'Race Meetings, Competitions, Dances and Cinema Shows' were also 'held frequently'.

Compared with the diversions on today's ships, this all seems very homespun and hearty – but perhaps none the worse for that. 'Christmas and New Year Tours to South Africa' by the British Union-Castle Line in 1935–36 offered similar choices, claiming modestly that 'not the least enjoyable part of a South African holiday is the voyage out and home in one of these magnificent vessels renowned for their service and catering'. Despite the obligatory reference to 'invigorating sea air', potential passengers were reassured that they could also 'lazily bask in the sunshine or [recline] in a shady corner of the deck' – and, should time drag, 'concerts and fancy dress balls' were 'occasionally held … to make the time pass.'

The fine passenger-cargo vessels of Alfred Holt's prestigious Blue Funnel Line, based in Liverpool, carried between 150 and 230 passengers in first class only, offering 'the traveller a very wide choice', from 'a 12 days' trip to the Mediterranean or Canary Islands to a 'four months' round voyage'. It was stressed that 'passengers may stay aboard while the vessels are in port, if they wish, so that no hotel expenses are incurred'. In addition: 'Modern Steam Laundries are installed in all the vessels, which are also equipped with a Library of standard and up-to-date works, as well as a Barber's Shop with a fully trained hairdresser.' The sense of community on such vessels is suggested by the fact that they often staged *Diner d'Adieu* on the last evening at sea, with all passengers listed on the menu printed for that occasion. It was the custom for passengers to sign and exchange menus as a memento of the voyage.

Permanent tiled pools eventually replaced rather grim temporary ones of heavy canvas stretched over framing, and *Orion*'s first-class 'swimming bath' was 'open to the sun ... [the] green sparkle of ever-flowing seawater ... deepened by the blue of the bath's floor'; the later *Orcades* also featured a children's paddling pool. Yet official publicity images from this period generally convey scant sense of enjoyment. It is true that ship movement prevents a large pool even today (though the forced currents of modern 'wave pools' now allow energetic swimming against the flow), but many early pools were decidedly gloomy by modern standards. Those indoors seemed dank (if sometimes architecturally imposing), while those on deck often resembled nothing so much as flooded cargo holds.

Amid the large-scale operations of mass cruising, some companies still offer an experience tailor-made for the expectations of certain groups. The British cruise firm Swan Hellenic sends its 702-passenger *Minerva II* on 'discovery cruises' all over the world, with a roster of more than one hundred distinguished guest speakers to provide cultural background on places visited. The British company 'Voyages of Discovery' targets a similar clientele, with a team of guests speakers that 'includes historians, naturalists, diplomats and ornithologists', but *Minerva II* is billed as offering 'discovery cruises, country house-style' – a phrase that indicates the lifestyle of its target passengers. The ship's Wheeler Bar is named for the British archaeologist Sir Mortimer Wheeler, who spoke on the first cruises arranged by Swan for the Hellenic Society in the early 1950s. It is described as having 'a club-like atmosphere [that] provides the perfect place to meet like-minded friends', while the ship's facilities offer 'the perfect setting for every occasion and your every mood', whether this be 'dressed for dinner' or 'simply seeking the perfect spot to settle down with a good book'. Unusually, some 20 percent of Swan Hellenic's roster of speakers is clergy (seagoing bishops are also members of the House

ABOVE LEFT This unusually shaped children's pool, located towards the stern, follows the line of *Canberra*'s hull. From the 1930s onwards, some cruise ships provided both pools and games rooms (often with trained nannies in attendance) for passengers' children. Modern vessels feature a range of entertainment, including video games rooms and onboard children's clubs (though some vessels do not take children at all).

ABOVE *Hanseatic*'s tourist-class indoor pool was located on the ship's very lowest deck, well below the waterline, to minimize water movement. Even so, the level is kept noticeably low, and grab bars are fitted. No doubt one could keep fit by swimming here, but it is hard to believe that the overall space was very appealing – certainly when compared with today's outdoor pools for all.

FACING Cruising need not be all wining and dining. This passenger keeps in good shape through using the generous deck space available on P&O's *Canberra*. From the very start, cruises had stressed the supposedly beneficial effects of sunshine and sea air, even for those of a more sedentary disposition.

of Lords), so that 'Guests and staff have the option of attending a service with communion on Sundays'. A ship is a world of its own, and in the case of *Minerva II* a very particular one.

Swan Hellenic is now owned by Carnival, which has tried – and abandoned – the idea of speakers on its own cruise ships, as it finds its guests already have enough to do. The vast indoor entertainment spaces on modern cruise ships are made possible only by technical advances in ship construction, and especially by air-conditioning. Key features are a dramatic central atrium, now an obligatory feature on any sizeable ship, and a large show theatre able to accommodate all passengers. The large ship's cinema space is usually replaced by more cost-effective TV and video in individual cabins (first introduced throughout on Carnival's 1981 *Tropicale*), but vessels typically have several live bands, as well as smaller musical groups. Most ships now feature internet facilities, and the 2004 *Carnival Valor* is the first cruise ship to offer wire-free access from portable computers anywhere aboard. Mobile telephone networks are giving increased coverage nearer to land; eventually, no doubt, the majority of some 3,000 passengers aboard will be able to tell their friends – loudly – where they are (more or less) at any time of day or night.

A major source of income on cruises is gambling, and ships boast well-equipped casinos, while state-of-the-art spas and wellness centres are often leased out profitably to specialist companies. At anchor, some vessels offer water-sports facilities from special stern docks, but much cruise entertainment does not relate to the sea. Indeed, with their inward-looking configuration, cruise ships can resemble many modern purpose-built holiday resorts. Such self-contained leisure and entertainment oases operate with little or no relation to their immediate surroundings, and often

ABOVE LEFT Seahorses. These ladies pose astride some of the extensive fitness equipment available aboard the 2001 *Carnival Spirit*. No cruise vessel is now complete without a full range of fitness, wellness, sauna and massage facilities. In this, as in other respects, life at sea increasingly resembles the good life ashore.

ABOVE RIGHT Large cruise ships have designated jogging tracks, so that even when in port – as here on Star Cruises' 1995 *Superstar Gemini* – it is more convenient to run round the sun deck than to venture into the woods just alongside. This setting neatly expresses the perennial attraction of the ship as one's base for the duration of the cruise.

FACING LEFT Fashions are almost as exciting as the shuffleboard in this 1976 shot of deck life on Costa Lines' 1967 *Italia*. Accommodation included 213 first-class state rooms, each with individually controlled air-conditioning, and the ship also offered a 'duty-free shopping centre, barber shop, beauty parlour, laundry, dispensary, convention facilities and six passenger elevators'.

FACING ABOVE RIGHT German-style bathing beauties pose around the first-class pool on the *Hanseatic* – though it seems cramped by today's standards, with lifeboats in the background. The design of modern vessels, together with their greater size and number of decks, means that passengers need never see such things unless they choose to take a walk on the lifeboat deck – and it is often deserted.

FACING BELOW RIGHT This 1971 cruise by German Atlantic Line's *Hamburg* included (for a fee) the opportunity to play at five golf courses ashore, from Las Palmas to Lauderdale Lakes, so such target practice on board was no doubt essential. The whole golf programme was overseen by German champion Hans Heiser.

feature accommodation looking onto a central artificial lake. The only difference with a cruise ship – and it remains a major difference – is that the resort moves.

The grand yet eclectic styling of cruise ships is uniquely revealing of popular taste – sometimes to the dismay of architects and designers ashore. Yet they are important cultural phenomena: mobile self-contained, self-selecting, and inherently transient communities that exemplify the rootlessness and conspicuous consumption so characteristic of globalized mass culture in the twenty-first century. Their detailed environment of leisured consumption is nowhere more obvious than in the ship's show lounge, typically located forward, which will today be equipped to the standard of a comparable venue on land: computerized laser lighting and sophisticated scene-changing equipment is routine, with entertainers trained to a high standard. Companies pride themselves on being able to offer guests a show equivalent to what they might find at a metropolitan theatre. Such pressure of supply and competition is good news for passengers – and the final selected talent is all included as part of the cruise.

Ship entertainment values also reach ashore: harbour areas of popular cruise ports are cleaned and sanitized, with 'colourful natives' often vetted and selected by local authorities to sell souvenirs in appropriate national costumes. Passengers in a small port can constitute a large percentage of the 'population' (in spending power they may well be the majority), and cruise companies may sign agreements with local outlets, and recommend passengers where to shop. The tendency is for tourists to 'consume' destinations as entertaining spectacles, rather than seeking to understand them as complex environments where real individuals live their daily lives. Travel publicity generally still tends to portray local people in 'native' wear, or engaged in suitably photogenic (but stereotypical)

activities. That such individuals may well be just as cultured as any visitor, or even more so, is perhaps still a thought that sits ill with the undoubtedly simpler appeal of sampling their 'exotic' culture in a brief shore visit from a large ship.

Most entertainers on cruise ships have tended not to be well-known, but rather individuals making their name. (Italian Prime Minister Silvio Berlusconi started his career as a cruise-ship crooner – and still sings occasionally.) Ever-increasing passenger expectations, though, together with the wide range of shows now available even at home with modern technology, make it likely that big entertainment names will appear more frequently on cruise ships. Cunard has featured stars as diverse as Shirley Bassey and John Cleese aboard the new *QM2*, and reports that this prestige vessel is attracting enquiries from well-established performers.

In the 1960s, British-flagged passenger liners offered live entertainment of sorts, but the performers were highly regulated. Cunard hired entertainers from the British variety impresario Bernard Delfont and, as members of the Musicians' Union, or Equity, all had corresponding grades of pay and conditions. The cruise industry is now largely deregulated, especially with regard to hotel and entertainment functions: musicians are often drawn from Eastern Europe or the Caribbean, while speciality acts come from all over the world. Comedians and compères are more likely to come from the ship's majority market, with American and British artists the usual choices; comedy crosses cultural boundaries less easily than food or music, and shipboard entertainment must not ruffle guests. British comedians seem to go down quite well with American audiences, but not the reverse. The prestigious Cirque du Soleil has performed on cruise ships, and perhaps illustrates the appeal of a visually dramatic act devoid of language and cultural complications.

ABOVE LEFT Pharaonic oversight. The scale and decor of the Pharaoh's Palace show lounge on the *Carnival Spirit* is intended to impress guests as they enter: the atmosphere and general provision is flattering, ensuring that every person feels special and pampered. Only advances in structural design, and air-conditioning, make possible such dramatic interior spaces.

ABOVE The Pharaoh's Palace show lounge stage in action. Provision for passengers to dance tends to be limited, as modest-sized discotheques have largely replaced ballrooms on most cruise ships. Changing social fashions apart, high-tech lighting and sound systems, once installed, cost less than an orchestra. Ships do, though, often feature several live bands, along with a pianist and small groups of musicians playing classical music before dinner.

FACING Decor to make you feel like an emperor on the *Carnival Spirit*. The central staircase of the Empire Restaurant features a statue of Napoleon at his coronation, while a corner of the Artists' Lobby bar is 'a great place to meet up with friends, or enjoy a before- or after-dinner cocktail'. Elsewhere, Louis XIV has a casino named for him, while Chippendale sets the style for the ship's llibrary and internet café.

New ships and high entertainer turnover necessitate constant recruitment. For example, Carnival auditions for entertainers as far afield as London, Sydney and Moscow, in addition to keeping an eye on shows in North American venues from Vegas to Toronto. Shows on board also change more frequently than at most land venues, and constant recruitment needs have led them to institute Carnival's 'Comedy Challenge', a local talent competition spanning the United States. Cruise passengers are also growing more demanding as the quality of home entertainment rises, and companies must seek out not only singers and dancers but also magicians, comedians and other acts.

Modern-day cruise-ship entertainment revolves around the 'show lounge' – a well-equipped space designed to accommodate different activities, and first introduced on Carnival's 1978 ground-breaking *Festivale*. The cultural origins of such a space lie ashore in the cabarets of inter-war Paris, Berlin, London and New York, where new large-capacity nightclubs, usually decorated in art deco style, aimed to attract prosperous urban sophisticates with a mix of dining, dancing, live music and stage shows. Performances were often thought risqué – for example, Josephine Baker's notorious late-1920s 'banana dance' performed as part of *La Revue Negre* at the Paris Lido (and reprised in decor for the Paris Hot bar on the 2001 *Carnival Valor*). Guardians of morality saw the very concept of a 'lounge', whether public or domestic, as suspect. As late as the 1950s a 'lounge lizard' was defined in Britain as 'one who loafs with women in hotel bars'; apparently, the very idea of 'lounging' offended conservative middle-class values, which always professed to favour work over relaxation (not to mention sex).

Ships in the British India and Union-Castle fleets had drawing rooms, smoking rooms and dining rooms that resembled nothing so much as *haute bourgeois* country mansions, or city gentlemen's clubs. The British company Royal Mail Lines boasted of its liner *Andes*: 'Wide promenade and sports

decks combine with spacious lounges and other public rooms to ensure the perfect holiday for both the energetic and the less active.' Officially at least, the choice was between the drawing room and the bracing air on deck, though unofficially it was known that on an extended sea voyage (chaperoned by her ever-watchful mother), a young lady might well find a suitably well-heeled match – whether 'lounging' or on deck. The longer the voyage, the better the chances, and vessels such as those on the Australia run were termed 'the marriage fleet'.

In the United States, meantime, the 'lounge' was fast becoming an established part of the middle-class suburban dwelling, in which comfort was as important as respectability. For household hints, Americans looked west to the idyllic lifestyle of California, especially as portrayed in Hollywood movies, and from the 1950s the informal 'International Style' of Charles and Ray Eames became widely fashionable in houses, motels – and new American liners. Aural comfort was equally important, leading to the popularity of easy-listening 'lounge music', which became the staple diet of the American cruise ship. Frank Sinatra may have invited listeners in 1958 to 'come fly' with him 'down to Acapulco Bay', but beyond the jet set it was in mass resorts like Reno, Las Vegas and Atlantic City that lounge culture blossomed. At the same time, the Latin music explosion led to 'exotically' decorated multipurpose entertainment spaces that brought echoes of Rio de Janeiro's Carnival to American hotel resorts.

Popular in shore hotels, a 'Copa room' also appeared on Caribbean cruise ships, once they became large enough to accommodate it. One of the first, the 'Copacabana Lounge', was installed on Carnival Cruise Line's *Festivale* in 1978, when the ship was converted from the 1962-built Cape liner *SA Vaal* (originally the *Transvaal Castle*). As built, this ship resembled more a fusty seaside hotel in very

ABOVE In the smoking saloon on DFDS's Danish-flagged 1964 *England*, the emphasis is on restraint and decorum. Although primarily a North Sea ferry, *England* was an elegant and well-appointed vessel built with cruising also in mind. She operated winter sunshine cruises from Europe to the West Indies in the late 1960s, though with limited success.

FACING The very height of fashion, 1969-style, on German Atlantic's *Hamburg*. The man with the horn is Jurgen Weigt, who led a quartet. In the nearby Alster Club, promises the brochure, 'the pianist sets the mood for a quiet drink together, while, in the Atlantic Club, one flight up, the Gents make their own very special sound.'

ABOVE A whole ocean of pool by night, it seems, on Star Cruises' *Superstar Gemini*; the lifebuoy indicates the true scale. The pool has become a focus for social activity on cruise ships, and modern vessels feature a range of bars and cafeteria nearby. In the evenings, an attractive pool area is often the venue for live music by one of the ship's bands.

FACING Attractive design, and attentive photography, maximizes space aboard this modern P&O cruise ship. A babe in arms enjoys the family pool, while in the background passengers relish the hot tub. Deck stewards now often dress very informally, as here – but are keen to sell drinks at prices that help maximize profits.

English Eastbourne (complete with drawing room) than anything likely to appeal to vacationing Americans. A US $30 million rebuild in Japan changed all that: a tiered show lounge was installed in the forward superstructure in place of cargo hatches and holds, so mailbags made way for mambo, and stylish glitz replaced dowdy chintz. There was no direct influence from venues ashore, and the performance space drew upon experience gained from converting a disco and storage space into a properly functioning theatre in the earlier *Carnivale* conversion. The company saw that shows and entertainment would be a central aspect of cruising, and understood that performers would give their best in a space properly designed and equipped, and with appropriate decor. That was the aim with the *Festivale*, within Carnival's financial constraints at the time. The name 'Copacabana Lounge' came afterwards, though obviously reflecting the pulse of the time.

A show lounge *is* sensory excess, and is not designed to optimize one particular activity. Recent cruise-ship show lounges have very well-equipped stages, as well as impressive lighting and sound equipment, but stage-audience relationships are compromised to some extent by other entertainment priorities. Seating, for example, must be comfortable and relatively informal (sometimes including sofa seating), and spread out enough to allow both audience movement and waiter service to small tables. Like the grand picture houses between the wars, soft seating and elaborate decor are all part of the larger show, flattering and exciting guests even as they wait for the performance proper to begin. Their luxurious surroundings reassure guests that, as they order cocktails under the glittering central chandelier, they are not mere spectators – they are part of the show.

Cruise ships aimed at niche markets, or specific clienteles, work on a quite different principle. They also have show lounges, but smaller than on the Carnival, Royal Caribbean and NCL ships. In addition,

they usually have spaces specifically designed for the enjoyment of classical music – such as the Curzon Room on P&O's 1995 *Oriana*, with its centrepiece Steinway piano. When this room was designed, builders Meyer Weft gave great attention to ensuring good acoustics. This was no easy task in such a wide, low space, but a state-of-the-art amplification system ensures that performances can be heard perfectly in every seat.

Most larger cruise ships have public rooms spread over two decks in the upper hull and lower superstructure. The atrium, linking maybe nine decks, will be amidships and, as on all cruise ships since *Festivale*, the show lounge is usually positioned forward. Most of the popular entertainment spaces are grouped between the atrium and the show lounge (casinos, shops, sports bars, discos and so on) while the more elegant and 'exclusive' facilities, such as the grand dining saloons, are located aft. Aside from dining and show events, passengers gravitate to that part of the ship in which they feel most at home, with the atrium acting as a piazza for everyone to 'see and be seen' in. In a well-designed ship there will be no 'dead' areas, or unpopular bars; if the range of onboard locales is correct – and correctly located, presented and staffed – they should all do well. The bar takings from different venues will show if this is the case, and are analyzed accordingly by companies; problems will be addressed at the ship's next refit, if not earlier.

The size and space of a modern cruise ship encourage passengers to organize considerable portions of their day themselves – though voyages can be plagued by announcements of planned onboard fun. On the other hand, for some locations (for example, cruises to Alaska) qualified naturalists comment on scenery and wildlife from the bridge when the ship is close to shore. Choice is part of the cruise experience from the moment one wakes up. Breakfast can be taken in the cabin (at a cost), in the

sunshine on deck, or in the dining room; times are flexible, too. If the vessel is at sea, the rest of the day can be taken up with reading, sunbathing, dipping in the pool, chatting in the hot tub – or undergoing a relaxing overhaul in the sauna and beauty parlours. Lunch can again be informal on deck, or more formal in the dining room, after which there is the agreeable problem of what to do until the evening meal and stage show. Options include shopping, or gaming and gambling, while for the more energetic there are tennis courts, jogging tracks – and on some vessels, golf courses and rock-climbing walls. Size allows greater scope in provision, and diversions on Cunard's *Queen Mary 2* include Cunard ConneXions, in association with Oxford University, the first planetarium at sea, and the Royal Court Theatre.

Evening is the opportunity to dress up (perhaps after a lengthy visit to the wellness centre and hairdressing salon), and guests sport a wide range of assorted garments, from smart casual to traditional – and even outrageous. Whatever the garb, the scale, lavishness, and dramatic lighting of the ship's atrium and grand main rooms can accommodate it. Music plays, cocktails clink, and the general air of conviviality is pleasantly contagious – even when only observed from an atrium balcony. Whatever passengers choose to wear or do, their entertainment value for others is assured.

For those who prefer the quieter life, modern ships have a high proportion of cabins with private balconies, a trend that, along with greatly enhanced indoor facilities, means that public deck space is less generous than on earlier vessels. Where once passengers could stroll on spacious promenade decks, today they can enjoy the small, but private, space of their own balcony. Even grand indoor spaces are related to facilities, such as bars, that enhance onboard profits; walking the open deck is still possible, but finding the door out to it can be a challenge. There is no profit margin on fresh air.

ABOVE These statues on Palladio's sixteenth-century church of San Giorgio Maggiore, Venice, have seen many elegant passenger ships sail down the Canale della Giudecca to the Lagoon, and onwards to sea. Here P&O's 1995 *Oriana* is handsomely framed between the church's cupola and the seventeenth-century church of S. Maria della Salute. The photograph is taken from the tower of San Giorgio, a favourite spot for cruise-ship publicity shots since it allows these dramatic architectural compositions.

FACING ABOVE LEFT In 1998, Royal Caribbean scored a publicity first with the 200-foot (60 m) high rock climbing wall at the rear of *Grandeur of the Seas'* funnel. Who would have thought that this could be part of 'going to sea' – but every other company will now have to match – or beat it. The largest cruise ship in the world at the time, Grandeur of the Seas also featured the Royal Promenade, an interior street 'wide enough to accommodate three lanes of traffic'.

FACING ABOVE RIGHT Casinos generate a significant proportion of onboard profits for cruise companies; once outside territorial waters, ships are exempt from the gambling laws of any particular country. This is Royal Caribbean's *Voyager of the Seas*.

FACING BELOW Despite all the electronic and other amusements now available on modern cruise ships, the simple pleasure of traditional deck games such as shuffleboard still has its appeal. Here passengers with P&O enjoy playing on a planked deck just as generations of voyagers with the company have done.

Dining

Cooking, serving and eating food have always presented special challenges at sea; and for some, dining at sea is impossible even to contemplate. In practical terms, the whole operation of presenting fresh-looking and tasty food at table demands sophisticated planning both ashore and on board, as well as a great deal of special equipment. Shore-based suppliers must guarantee both quality and prompt delivery (unlike a supermarket or hotel, a ship cannot wait half a day for oranges to arrive). In the late 1990s, the annual bill for provisioning cruise ships based in the United States was US $600 million; two years later, spending by the North American cruise industry was US $2.8 billion – with the total economic benefit of the cruise industry estimated at some US $15.5 billion.

Even a mere three-day trip from Miami to Nassau and back typically entails catering (rather differently) for more than 2,000 passengers and almost half as many crew. Over any extended period of time, statistics become quite daunting. In 2000, just some of the items consumed weekly by passengers on Carnival ships included: 53,314 eggs, 35,500 pounds of tenderloin, 350,000 shrimps, 61,800 hot dogs and 82,300 hamburgers. This was being helped down with 12,430 gallons of fruit juice, 11,230 gallons of homogenized milk, 307,260 cans of soft drinks, 55,480 bottles of wine, 11,925 litres of Scotch and 11,330 litres of rye and Canadian whiskey. Dining has always been one of the most important social rituals aboard ship, and on vessels with different classes, the serving of food (as well as its quality and presentation) remains a key indicator of ticket price – and therefore of status. A popular option on some modern ships is for passengers to pay extra for a special evening booking in an upmarket 'supper club', with fine food and wines and dedicated table service. Yet again, what was once the privilege of the few is now available, at modest extra cost, to everyone.

ABOVE 'The legendary Cold Table, groaning with asparagus and prawns, creaking with duck and poached salmon, bowed under the weight of profiteroles and cream.' Fred Olsen Line's 1966 *Black Prince* carried almost 600 passengers, and, in 1980, this 'Cold Table' boasted over one hundred different dishes.

FACING An evocative period study of black-tie dinner aboard Orient Line's 1951 vessel *Oronsay*. P&O, which acquired the Orient Line in 1960, gained its first mail contract in 1837, and its Royal Charter from Queen Victoria in 1840, playing a key role on the passenger and cargo shipping routes that maintained the far-flung British empire. Their ships carried everyone: troops, modest traders, eminent colonial administrators and prominent individuals from the colonies themselves. Lengthy passage times allowed for extended discussion at the captain's table.

LEFT The chef consults in the galley of the *Oronsay*. Modern ships' galleys entail cooking on an even grander scale. Dining-room orders sent direct by keypad technology and escalators for the waiters carrying food, help to speed service to the all-important passengers.

ABOVE Some of the contents of Orient Line's well-stocked pantry aboard the *Oronsay*, carefully laid out for the photograph. The tins here contain mostly Indian and other eastern spices.

RIGHT Menu covers could be very elaborate, often reflecting local architecture and culture in ports visited. This menu cover by Eugene Savage, from Matson Line's 1932 *Lurline* which carried 761 first-class passengers, is for Sunday, 30 December 1951 and depicts the annexation of Hawaii. Savage's menu series was awarded a Certificate of Excellence by the American Institute of Graphic Arts, and is held at The Smithsonian Institute, Washington.

FAR RIGHT A dinner plate specially made by Dudson for a gala dinner on P&O's 2000 *Aurora*. Fine fare here ran to six courses, from 'Wild Boar Terrine with Armagnac' to 'Exotic Fruit Vacherin with Three Coulis' – and coffee. In addition to producing commemorative items, there is a long tradition of potteries designing and making bespoke china for luxury passenger vessels, much as they do for grand hotels.

R.M.S. "MAURETANIA." Wednesday, December 4th, 1907.

MENU.

Scotch Broth

Boiled Codfish -- Oyster Sauce

Macaroni -- Neapolitaine
Mutton and Kidney Hot Pot

Roast Lamb --- Mint Sauce   Roast Goose --- Apple Sauce

Green Peas

Boiled Rice   Boiled Potatoes

Savole Pudding

Apricot Tart   Fancy Pastry

Ice Cream

Sliced Pineapple   French Plums   Assorted Nuts

Cheese   Crackers   Coffee

In earlier days, the whole enterprise of dining at sea seems to have been treated, at least on British vessels, much as imperial officials and their wives coped with tropical climates: no concessions being made for the difficult conditions. Menus from vessels of the past list what can only be termed 'demanding' dishes – demanding on the digestion, as well as on the galley staff who had to prepare them. In keeping with social custom ashore – and of course with the price paid for their tickets – passengers in first and second classes would eat in separate dining rooms. The poorest passengers, often migrants picked up at special ports en route, were in steerage, where conditions in the 1930s were still basic, with plain benches and steel bulkheads rather than ornate dining rooms. To save money, such passengers would often bring with them some provisions for the journey.

In the dining rooms, formality was the keynote: everyone dressed properly, and publicity brochures gave gentle but clear guidance. A 1959 brochure for the luxurious cruise liner *Andes* captures the tone: 'Although it is entirely a matter of personal choice, it is the general custom for evening clothes to be worn at Dinner. Informal dress may be worn in the Dining Saloon during the day.' As for children, if under the age of ten they would 'take their meals in the Dining Saloon at separate sittings'. After such 'advice', it would be a foolish or foolhardy individual who appeared for dinner informally dressed – let alone with a child.

Service was of a high standard. Tables were fully laid just as in a fine restaurant ashore, though such formality could always be upset by the behaviour of the ocean. Small rails, called fiddles, prevented dishes shooting off the table as the ship pitched or rolled, and chairs were often chained to the floor. Accomplished dining in rough conditions demanded a good sense of balance, a sure hand and a strong stomach, in addition to the obligatory grasp of etiquette. Part of the dining experience on such vessels

FACING BELOW Dinner offered on Cunard's 1907 *RMS Mauretania*, 4 December of that year.

FACING TOP Informal P&O catering on deck, probably in the 1960s. Such service was eventually abandoned because of hygiene considerations, but with modern refrigerated bars offering self-service, a rather more sophisticated version of it has again become a popular feature of cruising.

ABOVE A desirable window table in the dining room of the *Oronsay*. Passenger vessels at this date also carried cargo, and the view over the foredeck here shows mast-mounted cargo-handling derricks. Modern cruise vessels maximize revenue-earning passenger space with accommodation carried almost to the bow – where sometimes there is a helicopter landing pad (or a small pool for the crew).

ABOVE Some early menus were produced in highly original shapes, no doubt with an eye to their being retained by passengers as souvenirs. This banana menu made its appropriate appearance at a 'Tropical Dinner' aboard the United Fruit Company's *Toloa*, part of the 'Great White Fleet', 'At Sea, Saturday, 7 September 1935'.

ABOVE RIGHT Smart dress, copious drapes, and fixed smiles all round, together with chilled champagne make for a contented passenger experience aboard Home Lines' 1964 *SS Doric*, launched as Israel's *Shalom*, and subsequently the *Hanseatic*. When Home Lines sold her she became the *Royal Odyssey*.

FACING TOP One aspect of dining that all guests can appreciate on a modern vessel is the artistic presentation of food, as in this company brochure for *SS Doric* cruises to the Caribbean 1980–81. Elaborate ice sculptures are often a feature of the captain's cocktail party, which all passengers now have an opportunity to attend.

FACING BELOW The 1960 Russian liner *Latvia* was one of a fleet of nineteen similar vessels, each taking up to 333 passengers, built between 1958 and 1964. Passengers here dine in rather spartan – but determinedly modern – surroundings.

was the sumptuous decor, yet photographs of early dining rooms show rows of wall-mounted fans. No matter how good the stores, how talented the chefs, and how attentive the serving staff, dining before the 1960s (at least on British ships) must often have been stuffy and uncomfortable – especially in hot climes. It is hard now to imagine just how hot and smelly many dining areas must have been, and companies could do little but stress other virtues. A 1930s' brochure for the Jamaica Direct Fruit Line carefully described its ships as offering 'a very liberal and varied table'; and after the meal, the lucky passengers could enjoy that fact the some state rooms had 'hot and cold fresh running water'.

Whatever their practical shortcomings by today's high standards, the spectacular interiors of passenger vessels served as a reassurance against – and a distraction from – the elements outside. The very highest quality of food and service played a vital part in such reassurance. Passenger service on Hamburg America Line's great liners *Kaiserin Auguste Victoria* (1900) and *Amerika* (1905) was placed in the capable hands of the Ritz group. This seemed only logical since the Frenchman, Charles Mèwes, best known for designing César Ritz hotels, had been commissioned by the line to design the interiors of both vessels. (A meal by company director Albert Ballin at London's Ritz-Carlton Grill apparently led to this contract.) It was great transatlantic liners such as Germany's 1913 *Imperator* that were first dubbed 'floating cities' and 'moving hotels', and with justification. Not only did their first-class accommodation deliberately replicate the decor and dining of those exclusive hotels their wealthy passengers frequented ashore, it was designed by the same architects.

The tradition of fine cuisine at sea continues today, with the important difference that all passengers now also expect facilities for informal eating and drinking throughout the day – and well into the night. Ocean Village offers informal meals at any time on its ship, and all-day cooked snacks and a

LEFT A poolside feast on the *Flavia*, originally built in 1947 as Cunard's *Media* and acquired by Costa in 1968. Flavia operated out of Miami, offering cruises of three or four days to the Bahamas in what was by that date a growing cruise operation. This 1977 booklet stated that the ship served 'international cuisine with typical Italian flavour at [sic] your choice.'

FACING TOP This 1960 brochure for P&O-Orient Lines' new *Oriana* emphasized every aspect of her modern design, including here the tourist-class restaurant and its cutlery, which was 'ergonomic', that is 'moulded to receive the contours and pressures of the hand.' The ship carried in all 62,000 pieces of cutlery. Several eminent designers and consultants worked on *Oriana*, including Misha Black, Milner Gray, Kenneth Bayes, Brian O'Rorke, Ward and Austin, and R.D. Russell and Partners.

FACING BELOW This period postcard shows the smörgåsbord on one of Swedish Lloyd's four vessels, *Patricia*, *Saga*, *Suecia* and *Britannia*. Companies often provided postcards to passengers as a way of promoting their vessels and services, and some still do.

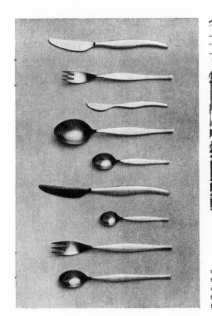

Tourist Class Restaurant

as "ergonomic", that is moulded to receive the contours and the pressure of the hand—and they are common throughout the ship. "Oriana" has, in all, 62,000 pieces, from table forks and fish knives to butter knives and pickle forks.

Tourist Restaurant
The discussion of good food needs comfort first and then tasteful but unobtrusive surroundings. Here they are as carefully thought out and designed as the full and varied menus.

17

late-night barbecue on the pool deck feature on many cruises, while Seabourn's 'Caviar in the Surf' is served with style by wading waiters. No matter how exotic the route, passengers can generally rely on good food cooked to their taste, with dishes from other countries and cultures (sometimes on special 'nation days') as a bonus – a far cry from the days when each national shipping line proudly promoted its own cuisine. In this respect, cruise ships reflect wider shifts in culture and cuisine ashore, where consumers are used to choosing from a range of so-called 'ethnic' eateries and restaurants. Cruise companies pride themselves on offering sophisticated dishes in grand settings, with decorative presentation dishes and elaborate ice sculptures featuring at cocktail receptions open to all passengers. A cruise ship may visit the third world, but life on board remains firmly in the first – and precisely that disjunction often subtly informs promotional images.

A combination of sophisticated computer databases and wide experience allows chefs to predict with uncanny accuracy what several thousand passengers will order for each meal. Cooking, serving and delivery facilities on new vessels are state-of-the-art, and are designed and installed as tailor-made units by specialist firms. A luxury cruise operator such as Seabourn will ensure that its chefs personally buy delicacies at local markets for preparation on board, and also that any specific food and wine requests from guests are met (wine and spirits are complimentary throughout their ships). Most ships, though, bulk load stores of all kinds by the pallet-load in their home port, though bread is freshly baked on board.

Companies operate their own training schools for catering staff, ashore and afloat, and run ongoing recruitment programmes in several countries for the cabin, catering and entertainment staff needed on new vessels. The crewing of large passenger ships has long been a world with its own traditions;

"Smörgåsbord" on board

ABOVE AND FACING Food as fashion. Passenger Peter Young took these photographs of the Midnight Feast aboard Holland America's 1993 *Maasdam* on a cruise from Vancouver to the Northwest Passage in May 1994. All the 'decorations' captured here are constructed from fresh vegetables.

FACING RIGHT Ornately presented cuisine aboard Commodore Cruise Lines' vessel *Caribe* (formerly the 1968 ferry *Freeport*).

FACING FAR RIGHT Cold chickens (with fan) perform under close supervision aboard Chandris Lines' *Britanis* in this 1971 publicity image: 'On occasions the Head Chef will even lay on one of his magnificently prepared cold buffets.' The *Britanis* was built in 1931 as the two-class Matson liner *Monterey* for service to Australia, and was bought by Chandris in 1970.

generations of 'Lascars' (from India and Pakistan) have proudly crewed P&O ships since British Empire days, while on some vessels the tablecloths and napkins are still laundered by Chinese staff, who have carried out this work for generations. For staff serving passengers directly, discipline and professionalism are essential, with the *maître d'hôtel* firmly in command – though in recent years the mass staff recruitment to match fleet expansions has sometimes resulted in less-than-perfect competence. Regiments of waiters and busboys are today recruited internationally by all companies – mainly from the Caribbean, Central America, the Philippines and, more recently, Eastern Europe. These staff are paid at much lower rates than unionized American or European crews, but – as companies emphasize – are well-paid by their home standards. Securing a job on a cruise ship with payment in hard currency enables many of them to send money home regularly.

After call centres and business-processing firms, global cruise companies are thought to be the largest recruiters in India (whose people are valued for their command of the English language). Indian hotel staff taking to the seas may increase tenfold their typical wages being about US $200 a month. Staff turnover is high, though, at around 45 percent, and most work at sea for only four to five years. Most companies also expect cabin and dining-room staff to augment their income with tips. Some provide detailed advice to guests (even thoughtfully placing ready-labelled envelopes prominently in cabins), with waiters lining up on the final evening to accept the cash. Companies argue that tips motivate staff to provide good service – and therefore (it is to be hoped) earn more, and in the pampered leisure context of a cruise, many passengers do presumably tip generously. Some companies at the higher end of the market, though, recognize the awkwardness that tipping can cause and stress that all tips are included in their fares. This is surely preferable:

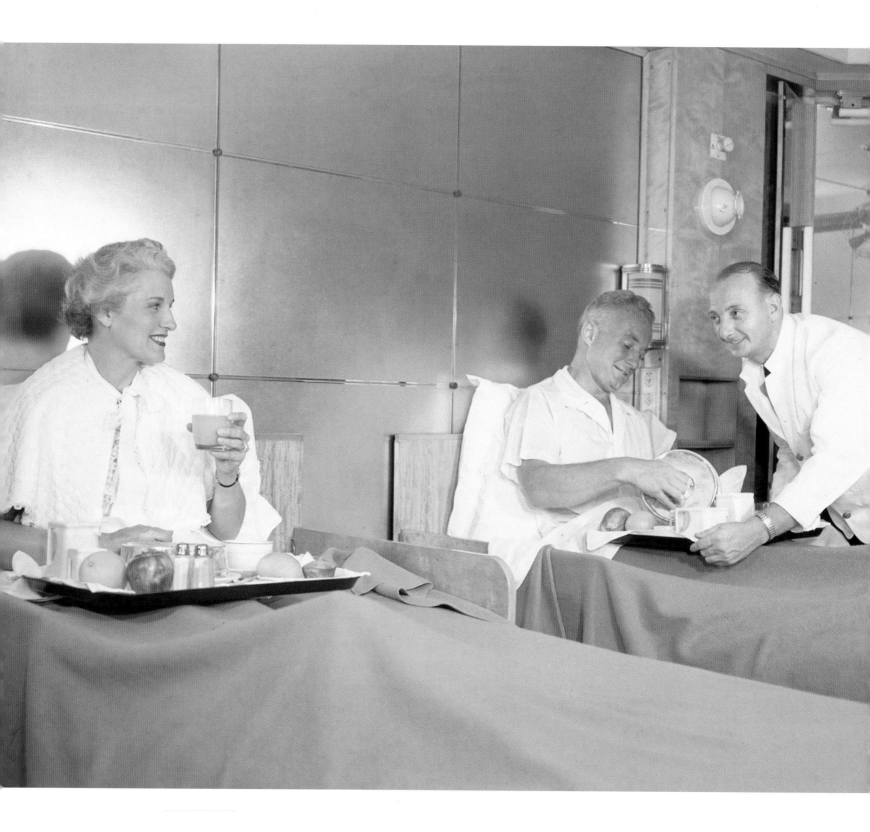

wages are paid by the employer, with the option that passengers may tip for good service, rather than feel obliged to do so.

Into the 1970s, ships of several national lines took great pride in their elaborate dining room service. Table settings were lush expanses of starched linen, silver plate and crystal, while uniforms were often magnificent, featuring smart mess jackets with gold braid and bib, traditional winged collars, highly polished shoes and hair clipped and combed to perfection. Italian ships were particularly noted for the attentiveness and flair of their dining-room staff, and for the skill and experience of officers. The Italian Line declined sharply during the first half of the 1970s, a period in which Carnival was growing, and it was to Italy that the Miami-based company looked (and still looks) to recruit its officers and engineers.

The international crews on the new mass-market cruise ships launched in the 1970s were proud of their jobs, and had a real incentive to try new ideas to make their passengers happy. On cruises aimed at the popular market, a certain showmanship in serving guests is desirable. Just as cabin stewards are taught to delight their passengers with cute animals fashioned from bathrobes, so waiters can display unexpected talents. Realizing that on short Caribbean party cruises every moment counted, and that dining was a highlight of the cruise experience, Carnival was quick to enhance the evening's entertainment value with staff trained to sing and dance in formation in the aisles between courses. So it was that the Italian singing waiter so familiar in the United States (though mercifully still unknown in Italy) took tunefully to the high seas.

ABOVE Seabourn's chefs take 'personal service' to new heights with what has become one of the company's trademarks: 'Caviar in the Surf' is served to guests when vessels are in port. Seabourn operates its small cruise ships almost as private yachts; each carries only 212 passengers but has 112 crew, with levels of service – and fares – to match. In this photograph from 1995, *Seabourn Spirit* was in Athens.

FACING Luxury breakfast aboard Cunard's 'green goddess' *Caronia* – at the time of her launch in 1947 Britain's largest passenger vessel. She carried 581 first- and 351 cabin-class passengers; there was no tourist class. Every cabin had en-suite bathrooms, and she boasted the first permanent outdoor pool on a Cunard ship. Make-up and coiffure here look remarkably cool and collected, for first thing in the morning, but perhaps the secret lies in that air vent and fan.

Design

The design, building and day-to-day operation of a cruise ship demands highly specialized skills. A ship must be thrifty in operation, yet offer attractive accommodation and facilities for passengers – it must also be good-looking. Architects, engineers, interior designers, artists, sculptors, lighting consultants and graphic artists all play a role in ensuring that a ship is enjoyable from the passenger's point of view – and, therefore, profitable from the owner's. Weight and stability are major considerations, while features and fittings must not creak – let alone come off – in heavy weather. Safety is paramount. The *Titanic* disaster brought into being the International Maritime Organization, which still enforces strict rules on lifesaving provision, on the use of fireproof materials, and on the subdivision of all passenger accommodation to reduce risks from flooding or fire. These constraints are constantly updated, and the ship's internal layout (its General Arrangement Plan, or GAP), as well as the layout of all individual rooms, must meet requirements. As a result of such design and service demands, cruise ships employ sophisticated infrastructures of which passengers see very little, unless they opt for a conducted galley tour to see the technology required for producing daily some 3,000 gourmet breakfasts, lunches and dinners.

At a purely practical level, the long and slender shape of a ship presents challenges quite different from those encountered in designing a hotel or resort on land. Moreover, good design at sea must take account of how a ship functions, and what the demands on limited space are, from cabins to passageways, major public rooms, galleys and machinery spaces. Lobbies must allow guests space to gather informally as they wait for lifts, or move easily to the dining room, and here the specific needs of serving staff must be reconciled with the area's overall appearance and its focal points. An attractive vista is important for guests on first entering the dining room and, if possible, also when seated.

ABOVE The Spanish colonial style
of the lounge on the Pacific Steam
Navigation Company's 1931 *Reina
del Pacifico* reflected her regular
service between Liverpool and
the west coast of South America;
to board her at Pier Head on
the Mersey was already to be
somewhere else. This ship carried
280 first-class, 162 second-class and
446 third-class passengers.

Specific planning and construction details of all kinds – both large and small – are resolved on regular visits to the shipyard while the vessel is under construction. This section explores some aspects of exterior and interior design, non-structural decor and detailing, and a range of issues from marketing to memorabilia.

The tradition for luxurious passenger ships to feature original works of art on board was established early on and, from the 1930s, Italian liners, for example, not only celebrated the historical range of the nation's art and culture but also showcased work by contemporary designers and artists. When the *Andrea Doria*'s career ended after only three years in July 1956, in her sinking off Nantucket Island after a collision with the *Stockholm*, she took to the bottom an outstanding collection of Italian art and artefacts. The *Studio* art journal had commented of the 1931 *Empress of Britain*, which featured work by a range of contemporary artists, that owner Canadian Pacific had 'succeeded in presenting to the world an exhibition of the concentrated efforts of British talent and British manufacture'. Cruise-ship operators today commission a wide range of original works by international artists to enhance ambience on board, and also produce memorabilia of all kinds to boost profits – and to promote their brand image. Costa Cruises has opened a centre in Genoa called 'C Dream' that features both the traditions and the aspirations of the company in the field of passenger shipping.

The artistic dimension afloat was once further complemented ashore by leading artists of the day designing and illustrating companies' publicity material. Such posters and brochures are now sought after as collector's items, capturing as they do the style of a vanished era. Public and private collections worldwide even feature such ephemeral items as luggage labels, menus and brochures, all of which were designed with an attention to graphic and corporate detail now supplanted by

ABOVE LEFT This picture of the
lounge on Cunard's 1923
Franconia, set for tea, shows the
attention paid to ensuring good
illumination by natural daylight.
The ambience is one of 'classical'
elegance – but with comfortable
armchairs. *Franconia* was
scrapped in 1956.

ABOVE RIGHT The dining saloon on
the *Franconia* was nothing if not
formal, far removed from the
pattern of seating at round tables
favoured by modern cruise ships.

anonymous barcode technology. (Luggage still goes missing, though, and some guests may attend the inaugural dinner on board in the super-cool attire of tuxedo and T-shirt.)

The major forces in developing the Caribbean cruise market were Norwegian Caribbean Line (NCL) and the Royal Caribbean Line. NCL's pioneering 1966 *Sunward* was designed by the Copenhagen-based naval architect Tage Wandborg, of Knud E. Hansen A/S, and her squared-off lines allowed unprecedented cabin standardization. Modest fares compelled these new ships to raise onboard revenues from spending in shops, bars and the casino – and small cabins encouraged passengers to explore the ship. NCL quickly ordered two larger ships of similar design, and by the early 1970s had four purpose-built cruise ships, all designed by Knud E. Hansen A/S with interiors by Mogens Hammer, working the lucrative Caribbean market. Externally, the ships were white with blue accents and, while no national colours were visible, brochures stressed the fine traditions and seamanship of their Norwegian officers. Everything else was described as 'international' and, to land-locked middle Americans, this may already have sounded suitably exotic; certainly the names *Starward*, *Sunward*, *Skyward* and *Southward* more than hinted at escapist trips to exotic destinations.

Introduced in 1968, *Starward* was the first Norwegian-flagged ship to meet American 'Method 1' fire-protection standards that specified the use of non-combustible materials throughout passenger and crew accommodation. In Scandinavia, it was more common to use the British 'Method 2' approach, in which non-flame-retardant finishes, such as wood veneer, could be used in conjunction with a sprinkler system. *Starward* also differed in atmosphere from the earlier (and very Scandinavian) *Sunward*, which had panels in dark wood veneer. The new ship boasted expanses of bright laminate, aluminium and glass fibre, smoked-glass partitions, brushed aluminium details and Eero Saarinen

ABOVE This double cabin on the 1936 Cunard transatlantic liner *Queen Mary* exemplifies the paddings of domesticity. Amid the homely objects and decor, only the porthole reminds us of the seagoing location.

FACING TOP Entrance to the first-class games room on Costa's *Anna C*. Originally built in 1929, this ship was completely refitted in 1946–47, and her new interior spaces designed by Nino Zoncada, for service between Genoa and Brasil and the River Plate. Most passengers were emigrants and all first-class accommodation was air-conditioned, together with second-class public rooms. The *Anna C*. was scrapped in 1971.

FACING BELOW Ferragosto is the main summer holiday period in Italy, and here Costa's *Anna C.*, sailing closer to home, offers a two-week August cruise in the western Mediterranean in 1953.

'tulip' chairs in primary hues. Just one week before *Starward* appeared, another Hansen-designed 'Method 1' cruise ferry, the *Freeport*, was delivered to the Miami-based Freeport Cruise Line. This joint venture between the Bahamas Development Corporation and US Freight offered twenty-hour short cruises to Freeport on Grand Bahama Island, and also carried freight trailers and some cars. The two ships shared the same Miami terminal, and a generation raised on TV series such as *The Jetsons* and *Bewitched* recognized these ships as fashionable hybrids that fused the international style with 1960s 'motel mod'.

Over the same period, Royal Caribbean Cruise Line ordered three new ships from Wärtsilä, a Finnish shipbuilder that became a leading producer of the largest passenger vessels afloat. Designed, built and owned in Scandinavia, *Song of Norway*, *Nordic Prince* and *Sun Viking* (all delivered between 1970 and 1972) were vessels of distinctive appearance. Although also designed by Knud E. Hansen A/S, exterior profiles by the Norwegian architect Gier Grung gave them an identity distinct from the earlier ferry-derived NCL ships. Integral to this were sharply raked clipper bows and lido decks sheltered by curving glass screens, but the decisive feature was a funnel that incorporated a circular cocktail bar protruding high above the stern sun-decks. Marketed as the 'Viking Crown Lounge', this innovation became central to Royal Caribbean's corporate brand – a registered trademark that made its ships instantly recognizable as it loomed over terminal buildings.

Like NCL, Royal Caribbean used Mogens Hammer to design its interiors, with each public room named and themed after a famous musical. The 'Carousel Lounge' in *Nordic Prince* featured a circular ceiling design with abstract evocations of fairground horses, while *Song of Norway* had a 'King and I' restaurant, encrusted with gilding, ornate lanterns and oriental-style murals to suggest the riches of

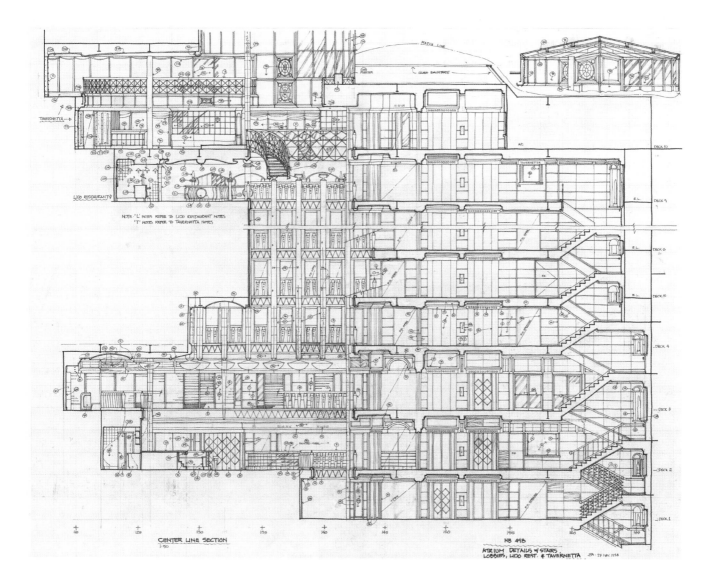

ABOVE A freehand drawing, to scale and covering ten passenger decks, by Joe Farcus for the 2000 *Costa Atlantica*. These working drawings also indicate materials to be used by means of different shadings, as well as including detailed practical notes on the fitting of myriad elements. Farcus regards them as finished works of art in their own right.

RIGHT A vessel for Holland America under construction at a Fincantieri yard in Italy, the country that builds most of the world's cruise ships. To speed up construction, large sections are prefabricated and lowered into position complete. Whole cabin and bathroom units are often installed in this way, which can allow for a different accommodation layout in the future.

ABOVE Norwegian Caribbean Lines' 1971 *Southward,* designed by Tage Wandborg of Knud E. Hansen A/S. This photograph shows her deck island and splayed funnels, the latter inspired by Costa Line's 1966 *Eugenio C.* The full-width lido deck on the *Southward* recalled that of the 1965 *Oceanic* – but without her retractable magradome. Since 2005, she has sailed as the *Perla* for Louis Cruise Lines.

RIGHT Norwegian Caribbean Lines' 1969 *Skyward* shows off her elegant and decidedly modern lines in this aerial shot. NCL's first fully-fledged cruise ship used the same basic design as the 1968 car ferry *Starward,* but with passenger cabins replacing the car deck.

Siam. This was a definitive shift: variety notwithstanding, previous passenger ship interiors had always referred to 'high culture' – whether Renaissance Italy, the grandeur of Versailles, the stately homes of England or, as on the 1935 *Normandie*, fashionable art deco. The new Royal Caribbean cruise ships took their cue from Tin Pan Alley, Broadway and Hollywood; for the first time the values that mass cruising shared with the most influential areas of popular culture were highlighted in ship decor itself.

The special design demands of cruising can be seen in the unique career of a Norwegian-owned vessel, whose sheer size also in some ways prefigured the move towards ever-larger vessels. The *Norway* was built in 1961 as the last real transatlantic liner, the *France*, and was heavily subsidized as a grand showcase of French technology, design, decoration and cuisine. When new, she was the longest liner in the world, but only ten years later was laid up as uneconomic. The Danish naval architect Tage Wandborg was eventually asked by Knut Kloster of Norwegian Cruise Line to assess conversion possibilities, the project went ahead, and on her debut at Miami in June 1980, *Norway* dramatically outclassed previous NCL ships. Her original 1,100-strong French Line staff was replaced by an international crew of 800, with Norwegian officers and thirty-two other nationalities represented. In her new guise the ship became a great dollar-earner for the Norwegians. Moreover, the US $130 million cost of her purchase and conversion would have bought a new liner only half her size.

For Wandborg, the *France* conversion 'was one of the most rewarding projects' of his career, and his strengthened friendship with Kloster encouraged both to think imaginatively about the future. Earlier NCL ships were relatively small, but *Norway*'s scale opened up new entertainment possibilities: a theatre big enough to stage Broadway-style musicals, and an impressive range of sports facilities.

Pierre PARRETON
Michel Lezla 61

ABOVE This cutaway of the *France* as launched in 1961 reveals the strict zoning of her interior – and also the considerable space occupied by her two sets of steam turbine machinery, necessary for fast transatlantic crossings. She was the last inheritor of a proud French tradition. Only one set of machinery was needed for modest cruising speeds (the other being left where it was), and two of her four propellers were removed.

FACING TOP AND BELOW These luggage labels for the French Line strike a distinctive maritime note in using the device of the company house flag as the main identifying feature. Launched in 1926, the *Ile de France* was the first of the great liners finished in art deco style. In 1958 she was sold for scrap, but made a final appearance as the *Claridon* in the 1960 disaster movie *The Last Voyage*.

RIGHT This brochure for the *France* emphasizes the French national colours, exploits the impressive profile of the liner itself, and also incorporates the house flag of the Compagnie Générale Transatlantique.

SS FRANCE

C ᴵᴱ G ᴵᴱ

TRANSATLANTIQUE

French Line

LE HAVRE/SOUTHAMPTON/NEW YORK

ABOVE The Capitol Bar aboard the 1999 *Carnival Triumph* dramatically illustrates how the reworking of familiar fluted column and capital elements by designer Joe Farcus provided a highly original ambience.

LEFT The Viking Crown Lounge on Royal Caribbean Cruise Lines' 1970 *Song of Norway*. She was built by Wartsila, and this innovative funnel-mounted room has suitably 'mod' decor by Mogens Hammer.

FACING ABOVE The elegant card room on the 1957 Swedish American Line's *Gripsholm*, with interior design by Nino Zoncada, including here Zoncada chairs by the Milanese manufacturer Cassina.

FACING BELOW The delightful Parasol Bar on Cunard's *Franconia*, built 1955 as the liner *Ivernia*, and converted for cruising in 1963. Interior design was by 'society' designer Michael Inchbald, who went on to create some spaces on Cunard's 1969 *QE2*.

Where earlier liners had shuffleboard and tennis courts, she could offer basketball and volleyball courts, as well as a golf driving-range. Her entertainment staff organized some five or six different activities at any one time, from make-up demonstrations, foreign-language classes, ballroom dancing lessons and exercise classes, to cocktail hours, chess tournaments and trivia quizzes. NCL also leased an island in the Bahamas for the exclusive use of its passengers, an initiative that greatly enlarged the leisure possibilities of cruising. With this dedicated destination as an option, *Norway*'s guests could now participate in scuba diving, onshore barbecues, and sports tournaments – or simply relax in a hammock between palm trees and admire their ship's impressive profile as she rode at anchor offshore.

At the time of writing, *Norway* is laid up following a serious boiler explosion; it seems unlikely that she will cruise again, thus ending a remarkable design story. Grand she certainly was, but the influence of *Norway* on the design and development of cruise ships is debated. Her imaginative conversion certainly gave new life to a magnificent ship, and the venture was successful financially; on the other hand, *Norway* can be seen as a splendidly opportunistic one-off – she became a cruise liner because she was there.

Passenger vessels of the *France*'s era were characterized by design that was essentially the result of restrained influences, one of evolution rather than revolution. Indeed, in the case of the *France*, it might be argued that this was precisely the problem; unduly influenced by tradition, the French government launched a large, and very expensive, white elephant. On the other hand, Home Lines' 1965 *Oceanic* beautifully exemplified the culmination of decades of sophisticated Italian shipbuilding and design innovation – and is still working today. The largest vessel cruising full-time during this period (though originally designed for summer transatlantic service), she was both majestic and

elegant. Her hull carried a long, low superstructure receding in layers, with lifeboats nested in recesses above the promenade deck and below the ship's most remarkable feature – the full-width lido area, which filled the greater part of the upper deck amidships.

This lido was protected by glazed screens on either side, and above by a retractable glazed 'magradome' roof, making it usable all year round. It featured two oval bathing pools in free-form mosaic surrounds, with shallow water in which to relax. Decking was in a 'crazy paving' pattern, like the terrace of a contemporary hotel on the Italian Riviera, with tables under colourful parasols and groups of loungers. This attractive area was a reprise of the elegant lido area on Italy's famous 1932 transatlantic liner *Rex*, but also the prototype for similar features on many later ships. Exclusive cabins abaft the bridge even boasted private verandas. New Yorkers loved the *Oceanic*, and over sixteen years she developed a peerless reputation for luxury with relative affordability, for good food, and for the warmth and charm of her Italian officers and crew. By the late 1970s, though, she was the only large liner sailing regularly from the city all year round, and in 1985 Home Lines sold her. Her artworks had been removed, and her Italian crew was replaced with largely Colombian staff.

The *Oceanic* exemplified progressive design and attention to the demands of the market. Only minor changes in building were required to make her suitable for cruising only – and she is reputed to have repaid her US $40 million cost within five years. Miller records that repeat bookings were very common, and that on one sixteen-day Caribbean cruise 793 of the 873 passengers were repeaters. Careful attention to the imaginative design of guest-sensitive details can endear a ship to her passengers. Such details include ensuring adequate mirrors and storage space in cabins, giving attention to corridor width and lighting, and to lift size and speed, providing clear and coherent

RIGHT The unmistakable smell of the ocean, French-style. The design of this bottle of *Voyageur* aftershave, from French manufacturer Jean Patou evokes the ever-fashionable art deco period, but dates from 1994.

FACING ABOVE Passenger-vessel shapes apparently hold an endless fascination for us all: this teapot, from the British company Racing Teapots (which also makes teapot cars), adapts an original 1920s design to feature the 1969 *QE2*.

FACING LEFT Ashtrays, each of the same basic design, decorated for use aboard Holland America's 1973 *Prinsendam* and Cunard's 1969 *QE2*.

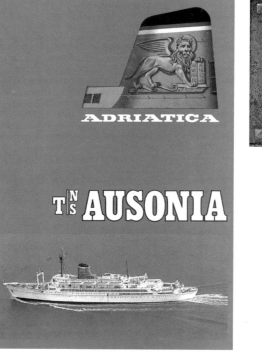

FACING Though seemingly diverse, the consistent element of these relics – advertisements for the fine passenger ships long ago put out of commission – is that they all stress the size and sophistication of the ships. Contrast the majesty of the vessels, and the companies behind them, with the depiction of the apparently innocent (and happy) 'natives'. From the *Viceroy of India* to the lion of the Venetian Republic displayed on the *Ausonia's* funnel, these representations of the might of the shipping lines conspire – along with the graphically simplified Caribbean history (this page, right) from the German Atlantic Line – to make foreign parts seem easily accessible and immediately appealing.

FACING BELOW RIGHT One consistent element in a ship's history, however frequently its far-flung destinations and its livery may change, is the bronze builder's plate. It is traditionally fixed to the front of the ship's bridge, and usually survives name changes.

RIGHT AND ABOVE RIGHT After German Atlantic Line's 1959 *Hanseatic* turned to cruising, advertising for her voyages became decidedly more informal and inclusive, as this 1964 re-working of the classic 'ship–shore' image illustrates (above right). The brochure stressed that facilities on board were open to all passengers and its playful cartography (right) offered up diverse cultures to be sampled, cocktail-like, as entertainment. The ship itself is our guiding compass to this apparently carefree world: 'Cruising the Caribbean is as colorful and varied as a world trip . . . European colonial cultures blend with the unique flavor of each exotic island.' If only history were so simple.

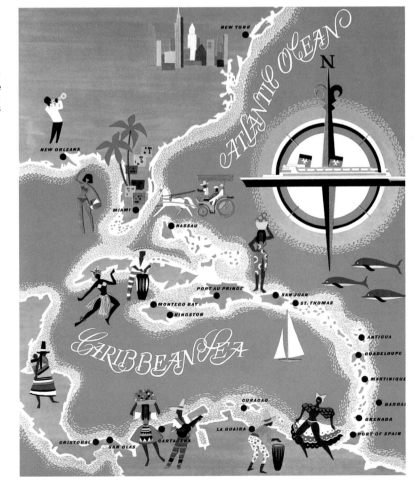

LEFT Mattel's 1997 'Carnival Cruise Barbie Special Edition' is kitted out in style for 'all the fun and excitement of her first ever Carnival "Fun Ship"® vacation!' In her fashionable reworking of naval uniform details she certainly 'looks her nautical best'. She also mirrors design trends discernible in some cruise ships: gift shops afloat stock items mostly designed to reinforce the brand identity of the cruise company. With Carnival Cruise Barbie, two powerful brands reinforce one another.

FACING After the success of his budget airline easyJet in Europe, Stelios Haji-Ioannou took to the waves in 2005 with easyCruise. As this publicity image from the launch of *EasyCruiseOne* suggests, the company's focus is on informality and fun. The ship is in port during the afternoons and evenings so that passengers can enjoy nightlife ashore. All bookings are made online and the ship can be joined at any port, so long as two nights are spent on board: 'Party in Cannes, wake up in St Tropez!'

signage (critical on today's large vessels) and ensuring that window levels and nearby fittings do not obstruct the view when passengers are seated. Any innovation that gives greater light (better still, a view) for individual cabins will be much appreciated – and so improve profitability.

The need for passenger vessels to be profitable, once government support was withdrawn, had a direct and decisive effect on cruise-ship design. By the 1970s, the only vessels not sailing as class-divided transatlantic liners in summer, and as one-class cruise ships in winter, were those from France and Italy, where state-owned transatlantic lines still received generous government subsidies. Ships in this sector catered mainly for the top end of the American and European markets, taking passengers who could afford the fares needed to maintain fully unionized crews at ratios of one crew member to every two passengers.

Most cruise ships exhibit a striking difference between exterior and interior style, just as was the case with earlier ocean liners. Outwardly, many vessels are demure, even bland, with emphasis upon a reassuringly elegant, if occasionally over-streamlined, profile. Traditionally restrained nautical design still exerts an influence here, and there is generally little use of decoration as such, with functional equipment and details such as lifeboats blended into the superstructure wherever possible. The smooth white shell of the hull and superstructure gives no hint of the fun palace within. Interior decor, by contrast, stresses rich ornament and detail, with central features such as staircases, chandeliers, sculptures and decorative flower and water arrangements all designed to flatter the eye. In this odd disjunction, cruise ships bear a curious resemblance to recent out-of-town 'leisure warehouses' and multiplex cinema sites, whose neutral box construction gives no indication of function (which is therefore proclaimed in illuminated logos and letters). Such 'placelessness' is one aspect of what has

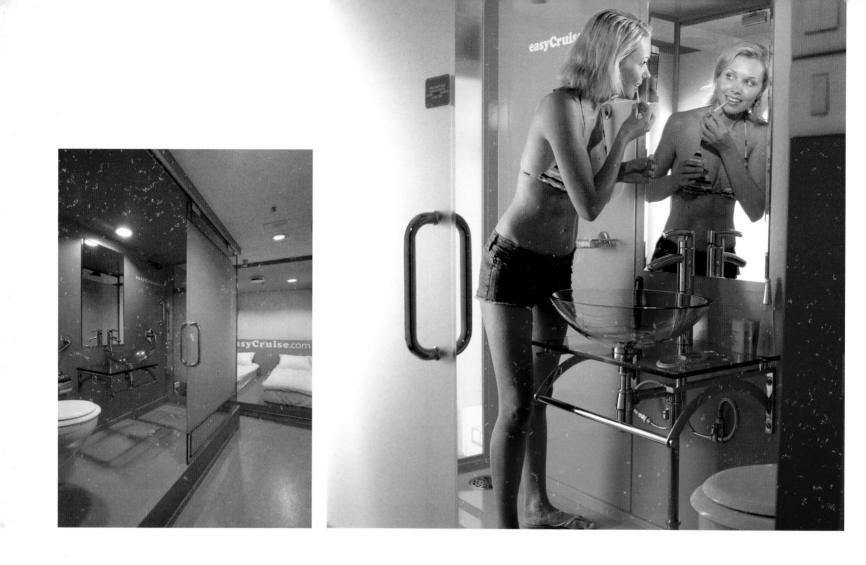

come to be termed post-modernism, and the inherent mobility of cruise ships expresses this quality in an especially intriguing manner.

It was in the United States that consumerism – the taste of the people, not the experts – came to dominate popular culture of the late twentieth century. Globally, culture became increasingly Americanized in reference and stylistic nuance, while retaining national and local characteristics. From the mid-1950s onwards, such environments attracted more open-minded commentary, though critics generally doubted whether they were 'good taste' (or were certain they were not). By the 1960s, though, it was plain that Modernist ideology lacked popular support, and that high-rise public housing, in particular, aggravated rather than solved social problems. A new approach to design needed to take into account why Las Vegas was genuinely popular while Modernist tower blocks – even when impeccable in theoretical terms – quite evidently were not.

Post-modernism approached popular design from the viewpoint of the consumer, rather than that of architect or designer. It argued that in order to appeal to a wide diversity of consumers, with varying ideas about 'good taste' and modernity, leisure and retail design should embrace a plurality of cultural and stylistic references: the concept of 'hybrid modernity' was born. A key aim of Modernism was to tidy up the world, and to create order and uniformity rather than embrace diversity and individualism. Post-modern thinking, by contrast, was flexible enough to include even Modernist ideals and aesthetics. It was during this period that the rapid expansion of cruising as we know it today began, and today's vessels still reflect many of these style issues.

Post-modern space tends, typically, to be self-contained, filled with diverse imagery, and removed from historical context; the viewer is entertained by an opulent and eclectic spectacle. Whereas the

public buildings and statues of capital cities should evoke strong and specific nationalistic associations, the post-modern 'gaze' is one way, with little or no reciprocity and devoid of specific meaning. Any message is blurred or contradictory – yet the viewer is seduced and stimulated to desire more. Publicity for such environments is typically vague, but aspirational – 'classic', 'contemporary', 'traditional', 'modern' and 'luxurious' are favourite terms. The aim is to be all things to all people, or at least to most of those all-important middle classes and, although the styles adopted by major cruise companies have varied, their target population is largely the same.

Once again, technology played its part in these shifts in thinking and practice. In the 1960s and 1970s, the jet age 'shrank' the world – at least for those with money – and brought different peoples closer together. This dramatic increase in mobility and cultural encounter is one of the most profound changes of modern times, and one in which cruising plays a growing part. Meanwhile, globalization in the political, industrial, media and military fields ('Coca-colonization' to its many critics) triggered rapid expansion in the catering, hospitality and leisure industries. Giant shopping malls and chain hotels, together with the resorts and casinos of Hilton, Radisson, Marriott and Holiday Inn, today represent bourgeois notions of luxury worldwide, and similar aesthetics shape the interiors of cruise ships.

The 2000 edition of the *Guide to Cruising* produced by Douglas Ward noted that many of the shops serving cruise ships in the Caribbean were the same as those in Alaska – but then, so were the ships. Ward also described large cruise ships as 'retail parks surrounded by cabins' but, even if this is true, the truth has an intriguing history. Retail and leisure can indeed be seen as sources for the interior design aesthetic of modern cruise ships, along with casinos, shopping malls and theme parks – but the

ABOVE The *EasyCruiseOne* was built at La Spezia, Italy, in 1990, and was extensively refurbished in Singapore after her purchase by easyCruise. Her typically Italian exterior shows innovative funnel design, together with integration of well-defined elements and the use of colour to emphasize length.

FACING Interior decor on *EasyCruiseOne* allows the trademark orange colour, already familiar from the easyJet airline, to dominate. Smart, functional and youthful style is the keynote here. The ship takes 170 passengers, whose average age is thirty-three. In 2005, summer cruises are along the French and Italian rivieras, and in the Caribbean during the winter.

ABOVE *The World*, launched in 2002, is a 'passenger' vessel composed completely of luxurious apartments with related leisure and communication facilities. Owners purchase apartments, and the vessel's navigation around the globe is determined by a combination of climate and of significant sporting and cultural events at or near a suitable port. There are 252 crew to tend to the needs of 285 residents and, as the publicity states, '*The World* is a ship that carries our luxury vacation residencies across the oceans and seasons to the four corners of the earth.'

ABOVE RIGHT Apartments aboard *The World* range in price from US $2 million to US $6 million, with annual charges of up to US $240,000. Typical of this end of the market, classical elegance is the aim with the interior decor.

FACING ABOVE *The World* not only tours our watery world, but is also marketed as being itself a self-contained living environment. Conservative good taste is the hallmark of design. This bar could be in a hotel or golf club anywhere; that is precisely its appeal.

FACING RIGHT Many large cruise ships have a helipad at the bow for emergency use; the difference with *The World* is that residents may arrive and depart by this means (sometimes, presumably, in their own helicopter).

inspiration comes from outlets and centres built in the latter half of the nineteenth century. Cultural commentators, from the French writer Baudelaire onwards, have seen Paris department stores such as *Bon Marché* (constructed in the wake of Baron Haussmann's radical re-planning of the city along modern lines after 1853) as the first temples of consumerism. These palatial retail buildings, floodlit at night, seductively presented a range of commodities in theatrical interiors featuring grand stairways, atria and open galleries on many levels. They transformed shopping into a spectacular urban experience, complete with live music, fine dining and electric light. These stores, moreover, were self-contained; once inside, consumers were enveloped by colour, light, movement – and goods. Buying – or even just looking – was family fun as never before. Light, leisure and elegance were all.

Paris was the great administrative centre for France and her colonial empire, and its new stores, restaurants and entertainments, depended commercially upon white-collar workers of the burgeoning middle class. This section of society has continued to expand within Western societies: it works hard, takes the most holidays, buys the most consumer goods, and has relatively high expectations from life – above all, it likes to have 'value for money'. The bourgeoisie's responses to modernity, though, have always been paradoxical, and today's middle-class family may inhabit a new neo-Tudor villa in suburbia, but drive the latest Chris Bangle-styled BMW. Similarly, their traditionally styled sofa may confront a TV set with plasma flat-screen technology.

Such seeming contradictions characterize all popular leisure environments, including cruise ships. Since the late nineteenth century, the design of popular entertainment and leisure environments has promised luxury and escapism – for a fee. Variety theatres, ballrooms, urban public houses, cinemas and department stores often mimic the styles of the French court at Versailles in the seventeenth and

eighteenth centuries, in flamboyant baroque and rococo. Publicity for sunshine cruises in autumn 1930 on the British Blue Star liner *Arandora Star* was typical of the time in promoting the liner's 'palatial public rooms [and] beautiful Louis XIV restaurant', and this style would last well into the postwar period. Modern interiors do not slavishly reproduce period opulence, but still seek to convey an aura of wealth and grandeur through ornate staircases, spectacular lighting and the mirrored space of a grand atrium. Cruise ships are palaces still, but palaces in which everyone is welcome, and their decor reflects this important shift.

At sea, the principles of post-modern leisure design are complicated by several factors. Firstly, popular taste evolves constantly– in music, fashion and hairstyles by the week, in other areas more slowly. Secondly, the Americanized global leisure, entertainment and hospitality culture often incorporates local elements. Just as the decor of the Bangkok Hilton will share features with, yet be distinct from, the San Francisco Hilton, so the interiors of the cruise ship *Norwegian Spirit*, carrying mainly American holidaymakers in Alaskan waters, will resemble but also differ from its sister ship *Superstar Virgo*, serving mainly Hong Kong Chinese passengers in Far Eastern waters.

Architects and academics have often found the Versailles-style aesthetics of popular leisure problematic, associated as they are with decadence, and with the ornate style of a corrupt regime overthrown by popular revolt. Indeed, the twentieth century has witnessed sustained tension between modernism's purist ideal of aesthetic restraint and style driven by the profit motive. A somewhat puritanical authoritarianism occasionally cites what is 'good for people' – but people have remained clear as to what they liked, and there have always been architects and designers to provide it. The distinguished British architect Sir Hugh Casson was not alone in 1969 in lamenting what he saw as the

bastardized taste of passenger-ship interior decor, although passengers themselves in all probability found such interiors both comfortable and comforting.

Casson's 1969 article, 'A Ship is an Island' for the *Architectural Review*, was written at a key moment in British passenger-ship history: the launch of Cunard's *QE2*, a vessel designed for the prestigious New York run but also able to cruise in the North Atlantic winter. Casson knew liners well, having grown up near the busy transatlantic passenger port of Southampton. He worked on interiors for the 1953 Royal Yacht *Britannia,* and for P&O's innovative 1961 liner *Canberra,* and his approach was shaped by a dislike of interior decor on many European liners between the wars. He felt that on them the 'dressing box of history was ruthlessly pillaged', their public rooms exemplifying 'a gruesome catalogue of architectural styles'. Especially he resented how, in the early twenties, 'new facilities were constantly being demanded' – a demand to which designers 'responded with a will'. The result was a series of 'Pompeiian swimming pools ... Byzantine chapels ... Viennese cafes ... [and] rococo cinemas.'

Casson started from the position, as the title of his piece suggests, that 'a ship is an island', but recognized the growing influence of American style in suggesting that, in the late 1960s, a liner's smoking room was now more likely to resemble 'a Californian country club [than] a Warwickshire manor'. Nevertheless, he rightly believed that 'the required atmosphere of being for a time in another world' remained essential to the interior design of passenger ships. Casson would almost certainly have disapproved of some of the excesses (as he would see them) of cruise-ship interior style, but it would be wrong to cast his own taste as simply conservative. The results of what the British architectural scholar Sir John Betjeman once termed 'ghastly good taste' can be hard to live with, and in conversation in

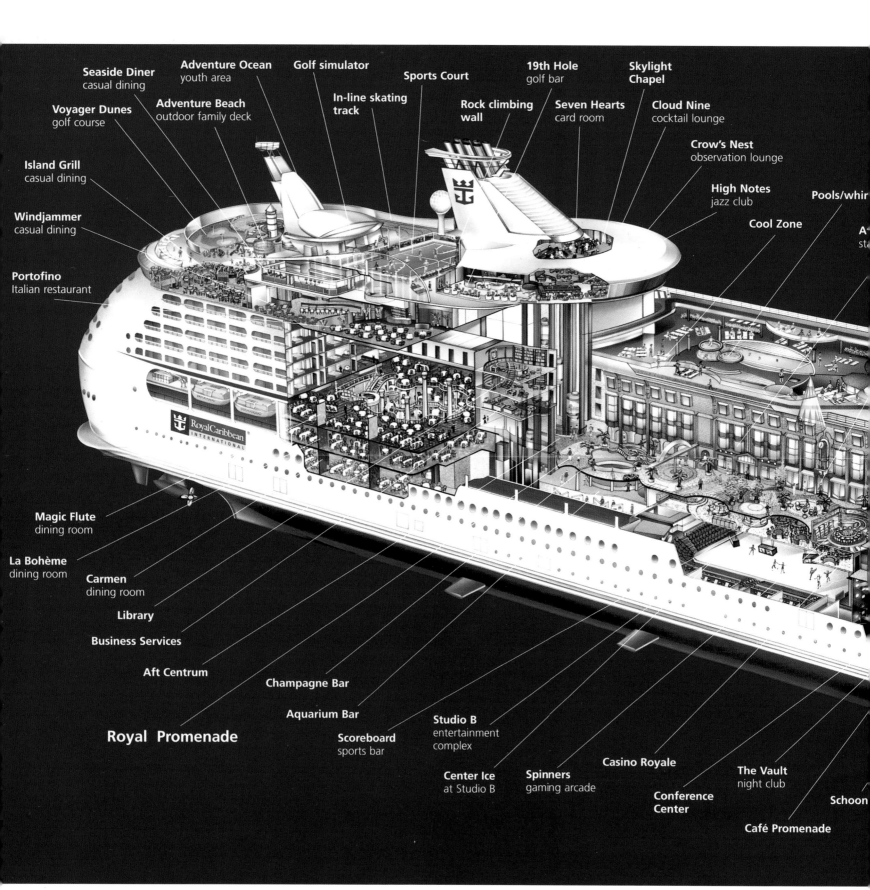

Seaside Diner
casual dining

Adventure Ocean
youth area

Golf simulator

Sports Court

19th Hole
golf bar

Skylight
Chapel

Voyager Dunes
golf course

Adventure Beach
outdoor family deck

In-line skating
track

Rock climbing
wall

Seven Hearts
card room

Cloud Nine
cocktail lounge

Island Grill
casual dining

Crow's Nest
observation lounge

Windjammer
casual dining

High Notes
jazz club

Pools/whir

Cool Zone

Portofino
Italian restaurant

A-
sta

Magic Flute
dining room

La Bohème
dining room

Carmen
dining room

Library

Business Services

Aft Centrum

Champagne Bar

Royal Promenade

Aquarium Bar

Scoreboard
sports bar

Studio B
entertainment
complex

Center Ice
at Studio B

Spinners
gaming arcade

Casino Royale

The Vault
night club

Schoon

Conference
Center

Café Promenade

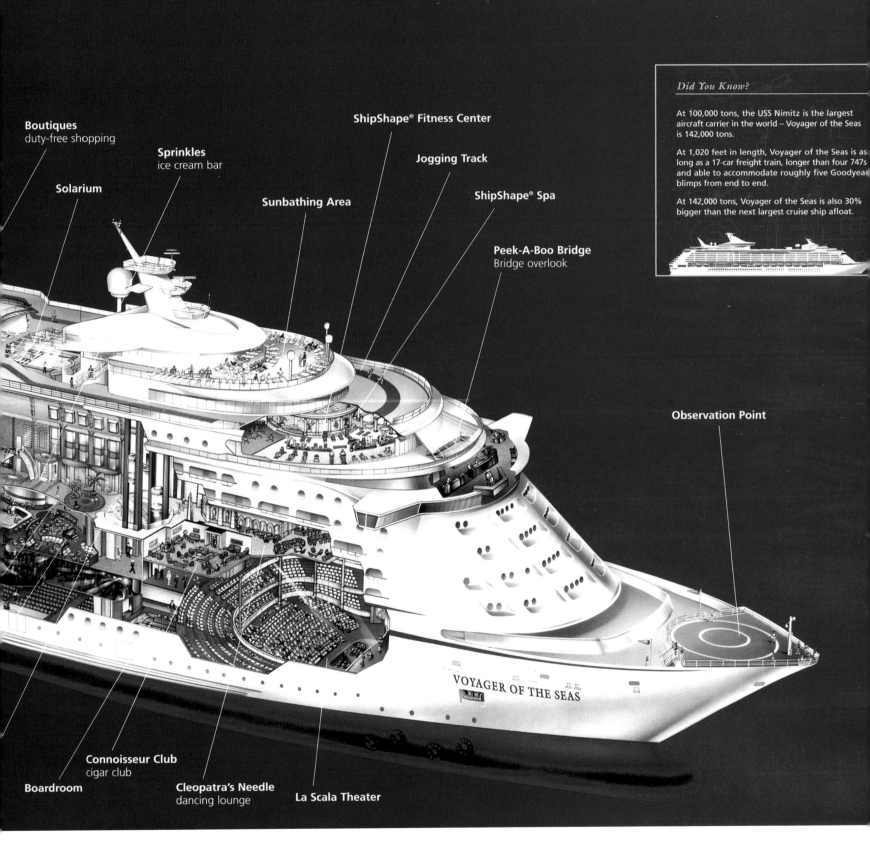

Boutiques
duty-free shopping

Sprinkles
ice cream bar

Solarium

Sunbathing Area

ShipShape® Fitness Center

Jogging Track

ShipShape® Spa

Peek-A-Boo Bridge
Bridge overlook

Observation Point

Connoisseur Club
cigar club

Boardroom

Cleopatra's Needle
dancing lounge

La Scala Theater

VOYAGER OF THE SEAS

The inside story of Royal Caribbean's 1999 *Voyager of the Seas*. Names are as important as what they locate on board, but this ship is designed and presented as a self-contained world, complete with beach, ocean and ice track – as well as a challenging cosmography composed of La Scala, La Bohème, Casino Royale and the 'Golf Simulator'. As for the world outside, the text declares: 'When Columbus found it, this was the New World, and now you can discover a whole new world of cruising with Royal Caribbean. A world where you can explore glaciers and steamy jungles, beaches and volcanoes, be plucked from one ocean to another, and be awed by the majesty of nature like nowhere else on earth.'

1993, Casson scathingly described some recent British cruise-ship interiors as 'the worst of motel modern'. His objection was not that they were modern, but that they were so unadventurous.

The taste and decor on cruise ships is determined very much by the market they target. Norwegian America Cruises considered itself an elite and exclusive company, and a former employee recalls: 'In the *Sagafjord* and *Vistafjord* we had the best cruise liners in the world, and both our many repeat passengers and the American travel organizations ... tended to agree.' The *Sagafjord* was the only liner in the world with a five-and-a-half-star rating, and she embodied 'the essence of a world cruise ship'. Carrying mainly Americans, she was 'a floating stately home for the old-money aristocracy of America'. Though the ship's striking interiors were modern Scandinavian in tone, they were on a grand scale down to details such as wardrobe capacity, and this last for a reason: 'You needed a vast wardrobe of clothes on such cruises.' The same company's newer *Vistafjord*, by contrast, was based mainly in Hamburg and patronized by wealthy German passengers. Her cabins were somewhat smaller, which meant she was better suited to long cruises, rather than the full-world cruises undertaken by the *Sagafjord*.

These outstanding liners, built in 1965 and 1973 respectively, were the work of Norwegian America's long-serving chief naval architect and technical director, Kaare Haug. Public rooms, such as the Saga Dining Room, the North Cape Bar and the Polaris Club, were created by a team of mainly Scandinavian architects and interior designers, many of whom went on to work in the developing field of cruise-liner interiors. Such work became increasingly specialized for several reasons. As passenger expectations rose and competition sharpened, cruise operators responded with vessels requiring ever more complex architectural servicing – ventilation systems, plumbing for cabins with en suite

facilities, advanced catering facilities and high-tech interior lighting effects – while still meeting the demands of ever more stringent safety legislation. In the past, shipping lines had employed architects and interior designers already noted for their work on land, but cruise ship outfitting now became a highly skilled professional field in itself. The names of leading designers such as Njål Eide, Joe Farcus, Mogens Hammer, Finn Nilsson and Robert Tillberg are legendary within shipping circles, but unknown to the public. These specialists work internationally but keep discreet profiles, and for them success is determined by the unforgiving yardstick of corporate profitability.

While NCL, Royal Caribbean and Carnival were expanding in the Caribbean, Greek entrepreneurs such as the Kavounides and Typaldos brothers, Dimitri Chandris, and especially Tassos Potamianos, were developing cruising in the Mediterranean. They purchased small and economical elderly tonnage for conversion, but imagination was essential since finance to build new tonnage was hard to come by – not least because Greece was then a military dictatorship. Indeed, only one new Greek cruise ship was constructed during the 1970s, Pericles Panagopoulos' upmarket and elegant *Golden Odyssey* (1974), designed by Knud E. Hansen A/S and built at Helsingør, Denmark. Panagopoulos was an enthusiastic collector of modern art, and employed a young Greek abstract painter named Michael Katzourakis to decorate the bulkheads with psychedelic murals. The combination of colourful modernist furniture and 'flower power' themes became the essence of Greek cruise decor of the period; *Golden Odyssey*'s interiors were much imitated, and Katzourakis established himself as an interior-design specialist, going on to decorate several, mainly Greek-owned, vessels. So skilled did Greeks become at conversions to meet growing demand that there were few ship types that the repair yards at Perama and Keratsini could not somehow transform for cruising: North Sea ferries, Thames excursion

ABOVE LEFT Long expanses of open deck were a feature of classic liners, and here P&O's 1961 *Canberra* retains that tradition. On modern ships, deck space is increasingly given over to rows of sunbeds, or to organized sport, but the lifeboat deck, being partly in shade, remains free space for walking.

ABOVE RIGHT Clean, if somewhat spartan, nautical design on Black Sea Shipping Company's *Maxim Gorky* (built as the 1969 *Hamburg*, and purchased in 1973).

FACING TOP Design on a ship must always take account of safety in all operating conditions. These deck windows on the 2003 *Costa Mediterranea* have central reinforcement, and are of toughened glass: in safety terms, a continuation of the vessel's upper steel shell. Doors and windows on ships often have rounded shapes to avoid metal surfaces cracking at the corner. The traditional porthole is perfectly shaped for its purpose, but cruise passengers expect more expansive views.

FACING BELOW All cruise ships have a functional, 'nautical', dimension with winches and ropes operated by the crew when docking and setting sail. On modern vessels these work decks are invisible to passengers; here, on the *Canberra*, the large open foredeck is arranged in traditional fashion. This area was closed to passengers.

ABOVE A low-angle bow view flatters a ship, and here the 2003 *Diamond Princess*, operated by P&O Princess Cruises, shows off her lines. The working crew area at the bow is neatly concealed (and sheltered) by a false deck. The dramatic bridge wing is essential for good sight lines on such a large vessel.

FAR LEFT Clean lines on the bridge of Cunard's combined transatlantic liner and winter cruise ship, *Queen Elizabeth 2*.

LEFT The open bridge wings on the *Canberra* were late examples of traditional nautical design in this area. Modern ships usually have fully enclosed bridge areas, with all-round visibility ensured by generous windows (including some in the floor of the bridge wings). There are sometimes also remote CCTV cameras bow and stern, monitored from the bridge.

RIGHT The *Diamond Princess* shows her other side: straight-lined multiples of standard-size cabins, with a table and two chairs on every balcony. Outside cabins command the highest prices, and designers exercise great ingenuity in ensuring that each vessel offers the highest proportion possible – and yet still looks good.

boats, yachts, cattle transporters, emigrant liners, and even redundant oil tankers, were all given completely new lives. As well as increased accommodation and new lido decks, many vessels were also given radically restyled profiles in an idiosyncratic and distinctly Greek modernistic idiom – the same style, in fact, that shaped countless white-painted concrete hotel resorts then springing up along the shores of the Aegean.

Surprising as it seems now, cruising under the hammer and sickle became increasingly popular in the 1970s as Russia's Black Sea Shipping Company built up a fleet of new and second-hand tonnage with a view to earning much-needed hard currency from Western charters. The Cunard vessels *Franconia* and *Carmania* were acquired as the *Fedor Shalyapin* and *Leonid Sobinov*, while the luxurious *Hamburg* became the Soviet flagship *Maxim Gorky* – and was promptly chartered by German tour operators, for whom she continues to cruise as one of the last large steam turbine ships. Soviet liners offered good value for money and a clean and orderly (if somewhat austere) environment. The food never approached the haute cuisine found on Western liners, and entertainment was often rather homespun, but many itineraries were imaginative – and the bar tariffs certainly more than reasonable.

Despite the Cold War being at its height, in the 1970s the Soviets even broke into the American cruise market with the purpose-built *Odessa*, a small liner designed by Tage Wandborg which was acquired directly from her British builder. By the 1980s, Russia had the most extensive and diverse cruise fleet in the world, much of it (ironically for a Marxist-Leninist state) aimed at the bourgeois Western leisure market. But the collapse of Communism and the disintegration of the Soviet empire, together with subsequent turbulence (and corruption) in the Russian economy, caused the entire fleet

to be scattered, and eventually sold off. In retrospect, it seems only logical that the lion's share of the twenty-first-century cruise market should be held by a company based in sunny Miami rather than snowy Moscow, and whose funnel shape and colours proclaim just fun rather than socialist ideals. But it might have been very different.

The Norwegians had built new ships specifically for the Caribbean cruise trade, whereas Carnival commenced operations in 1972 with the former Canadian Pacific transatlantic liner *Empress of Canada*, which was hastily converted into the *Mardi Gras* with only a cursory repaint and the fitting of slot machines. This was the first liner-sized vessel to be deployed on Caribbean cruising (two more conversions would follow), but Carnival had neither time nor money to devise its own livery, and instead adapted Canadian Pacific's 1968 'multimark' logo, which was repainted from shades of green and white to a more colourful red, white and blue. When the ship's former owner protested, the logo was adjusted to a white crescent between the red and blue. This livery has proven one of the most successful, and the futuristic winged funnel introduced on the company's first brand-new ship, the 1982 *Tropicale*, carried the logo also on the wing's upper surface, for the benefit of low-flying jets and wishful high-rise office workers in ports she visited.

It was Carnival that made the all-important breakthrough of convincing America's aspiring middle class to sail on its growing Miami fleet. Selling mass fun ensured its success. Cunard had stressed the uncertain 'fun' of an Atlantic crossing for the leisured and relatively wealthy, and back in the 1960s, Ed Stephan's Miami-based Yarmouth Cruise Line had used the tag 'Fun Ships' for its two vessels shuttling back and forth to Nassau. However, Carnival's operation was on an altogether more imaginative and ambitious scale. It saturated the potential American market with the concept of 'fun'

LEFT The centrality of the atrium to the overall interior design of a cruise ship encourages designers to excel in whatever style is chosen. Spanning several floors, and topped with a glass dome, this is the atrium on Royal Caribbean's 1998 *Vision of the Seas*. The designers were Njål Eide, Howard Snoweiss, Per Hoydahl, Lars Iwdal and Tom Grabowski.

FACING The Animator's Palette restaurant featured on *Disney Wonder* celebrates the skills of cartoon animators in 'bringing to life' static monochrome drawings. The lighting of the space starts in monochrome, then slowly changes in colour, with patterns also moving on the walls. This unique animated approach to ship decor illustrates – quite literally – how concerned Disney was to ensure the integration of the ships with an identity already familiar to their public from film and related Disney media.

afloat, and in 1984 was the first cruise company to advertise on network TV – an initiative recalled in current company publications. A typical TV advertisement might feature lines of female singers with big hairdos, sequinned dresses and gold-plated jewellery singing to a disco beat, 'Ain't got much money / But, oh, Honey / We've got the Fun!', and when its ships were in port, blimps bearing the same slogan flew overhead. Such tactics breached all conventional wisdom on cruise marketing – but they worked, and Carnival continues to use television campaigns to great effect.

Interestingly, Carnival had been offered the *France*, but decided against a conversion project on the basis of likely profit margins (a decision it repeated later with the transatlantic liner *United States*). Instead, they applied lessons learned from the conversion in 1978 of the South African liner SS *Vaal* into its successful *Festivale*. Farcus sees this Carnival vessel, at the time the largest Caribbean cruise ship, as the first example of ship as destination: 'All of today's innovations and gimcracks began there.' Whatever the verdict, between 1990 and 1998 Carnival launched an unprecedented (and still unequalled) series of eight *Fantasy*-class cruise ships, before going on to launch far larger vessels of the *Destiny* and *Spirit* classes. Unlike some rivals, Carnival has also avoided buying or leasing islands as part of its cruise portfolio, concentrating instead on its proven talents for designing and operating popular ships. On its commercial record, few could argue with the decision.

Carnival's nimble corporate structure gives Farcus unusual scope as sole designer of its ships, and this confidence has been repaid with a series of vessels distinct from all others. He began his career in the architectural office of American architect Morris Lapidus, designer of such innovative Miami Beach hotels as the 1948 Sans Souci, the Fontainebleau Hotel, now the Fontainebleau Hilton, and Eden Roc (both 1954), and has now designed well over twenty ships for Carnival. His interior designs

typically feature high-profile elements that would probably be toned down in any committee structure. Other designers, whose proposals are vetted at a series of planning meetings over several months, envy his freedom to send detailed freehand designs, drawn to scale, direct to the shipyard. He regards these drawings as finished creations in their own right, but they must also be informative, and demonstrate efficient and practical use of space and materials. As Micky Arison himself points out, having everything designed by Farcus – where typically various design committees would need to consult – saves Carnival time and money.

Since the late 1980s Farcus has approached his work as 'entertainment architecture', seeing it as his task 'to design an experience rather than just designing the materials'. Cinema has influenced his thinking, but he also sees himself as a traditionalist, bringing alive the unique experience of being at sea:

> The view from a ship is all horizon, with occasional terra firma drifting by. The stars are brighter at night than in the city. The floor moves! The service provided by the crew is at a high level seldom found at hotels. What a fantastic set of ground rules to begin a design.

A fascination with ships since childhood informs his work, but so does a hard-nosed understanding that any design must *work*: 'The cruise line signs my contract and pays the fees, but the passengers are the real clients. Satisfying their needs first is the best way to serve the owners.' In the early days, Micky Arison himself worked for a spell at sea as a Carnival steward, and still likes to steal away to sea when time allows. Understanding the way a ship functions is crucial, and Arison still makes a point of visiting each ship in the fleet once a year, discussing operations with senior staff from every section. When Carnival acquired Costa, Farcus was quick to cruise on the company's ships to assess both the

ABOVE On a cruise, indulgence is all, and these seats in the Oasis Spa High on P&O's 2004 *Arcadia* are an invitation to be pampered.

FACING TOP In the Atrium high on the *Arcadia* cool, modern sophistication is the keynote. Design and decor are restrained, in keeping with the company's traditional and proud image of British good taste.

FACING BELOW At sea, *Arcadia* cuts a fine image, with hull and funnel colours that evoke many decades of P&O tradition. Comparison with earlier P&O vessels, though, shows the extent to which passenger accommodation on modern cruise vessels now occupies almost all the hull, dramatically altering the ship's overall profile.

ships and the market. The profitability of his new ships for Costa has exceeded expectations, and larger ones are planned.

Carnival's approach and designs have played well on the new ships for Costa, and the Italian cruise line is now the fastest-growing element of its overall cruise business. Previous Costa ships had been sailing showcases for the very best of Italian design in a somewhat severe tradition that placed great emphasis upon clarity and restraint. The ships themselves, though, did not benefit from the best design knowledge in terms of layout and passenger flows, though they were always striking in appearance and included fine set pieces of architectural design. As always, however, a successful cruise ship has to be more than an elegant hotel that floats, and Carnival's operating and design expertise brought to Costa the know-how and imagination that have transformed the company. The success of the change is also a measure of the appetite for such ships in the Mediterranean, and especially in Italy; Florida-style fun clearly has real appeal and, though decor on the ships does draw inspiration from Italian themes, it is the excitement of the new world of America, rather than deference to tradition, that sets the style.

In complete contrast to such mass-market decor, some very few passengers determine the style of the cruise vessel themselves: they own it. The demand for luxury motor yachts is growing fast, and they are becoming larger and more expensive. Most such yachts are offered in a series of hull sizes and basic configurations, but interior decor is often chosen by the owner. Some extremely expensive yachts are designed and built entirely as one-offs, and such super-luxury vessels demand a very high level of construction expertise. They are the latest examples of an individually tailored aspect of luxury cruising that has, over the centuries, produced some of the world's most beautiful ships.

The remarkable popularity of cruising is a fascinating cultural phenomenon. In his book, *Place*, published in 2004, the distinguished British architect Sir Terry Farrell recalls his youthful crossing to New York in 1962 on the *Queen Mary*. For him, this vast ship was 'more of a floating village or small town than a boat ... It was an entire floating world of compressed life'. Farrell had researched artificial island habitations, and the liner fascinated him as 'a megascaled mono-functional container' akin to an opera house of sports stadium – 'but with all the features that go with being a "vehicle"'. As an architect he was intrigued by the disparate functions that are resolved in the design of an ocean-going vessel, especially the 'specialized functioning' of 'the 'container itself' with the 'ordinary human activities' in public, private and residential areas: 'All of this, unlike a naturally grown urban habitat, is designed and built in the specialized construction workplace of a shipyard, and then fixed in time'. Despite changes in passenger travel by sea in recent years, Farrell's insights remain true. They also suggest ways to see the ships explored in this book as part of mainstream design and cultural debate; time will tell if this occurs.

Few large ships of any kind survive beyond a working life of some thirty years or so, and therefore those that do are especially important. Returning to see the *Queen Mary*, static now as a hotel and tourist attraction at Long Beach, in 2002, with his eighteen-year old daughter, Farrell made a surprising, but appropriate, comparison between the great liner and an archaeological site. He noted how the design of the liner enabled 'various social classes to be kept apart for many days, creating a kind of floating apartheid, albeit a benign and voluntary one based on the price you could pay'. For him: 'The *Queen Mary* (like the uncovered Pompeii) conveys as much about society and its values at a point in time as it does about a form of transport.'

ABOVE The naming of the *Costa Atlantica* in Venice, 2000. Balloons representing the four winds carry figures past the ship, while acrobats abseil down the side of the vessel. The Madrina (Godmother) who named the new ship was Claudia Cardinale. Representatives from the builders and owners, together with the designer, officials from other shipping companies, and assorted invited guests (including the Vatican's bishop for tourism), attended this ceremony, at which the ship was officially handed over by the builders to her captain and crew.

FACING TOP In this picture of *EasyCruiseOne* in dock laser lighting emphasises her dramatically splayed funnel design.

FACING LEFT The great height of modern cruise ships gives scope for spectacular displays by acrobats and other performers as part of the naming ceremony of *Arcadia*.

OVERLEAF The beautifully designed 1965 *Oceanic* still makes a fine picture, even after forty years. Her elegant and judicious blend of function and form still represents what many regard as the best in passenger ship design.

ABOVE Cunard's 1936 *Queen Mary* made her final voyage (on only two of her four propellers) to Long Beach, California, arriving December 1967. After expenditure of some $US 41 million, she opened in May 1971 as a hotel and tourist attraction. This is a publicity image from that period: 'Gloria Newton sports a natural Afro-cut and is one of seventy-five official tour guides on board.' The handsome brass engine telegraph seen here, and even the traditional ship's wheel, are replaced on modern ships by small toggle levers operated from a comfortable driving seat.

FACING The essence of nautical style. This picture, aboard Norwegian Cruise Line's *Norway* (built 1961 as the *France*), captures the perennial appeal of ships for architects and designers – and, not surprisingly, nautical details look their best on board ship, with sun, sea and sky as setting. Nevertheless, designers must ensure that every detail of a ship functions efficiently, whatever the weather.

Acknowledgements

Special thanks go to Laurence King, Philip Cooper, and above all to Jessica Spencer, the book's Project Manager at Laurence King Publishing, for transforming an idea into the reality of this book. Keith Lovegrove's commitment and design skills have also been integral to its development. Laurence Dunn and Clive Harvey gave generous access to their archives. We wish to thank the following people whose encouragement, advice or help made this book possible, and also the many others who kindly loaned material that was not used:

Margaret Adamic (Disney Publishing Worldwide); Jane Allan (Glasgow School of Art); Alastair Arnott and Rachel Wragg (Southampton Arts and Heritage Services); Tilly Ashton; Kate Bates (P&O Cruises); Aly Bello-Cabreriza and Vance Gullikson (Carnival Cruise Lines); Jacey Bunker (Mattel UK); David Buri (Glasgow School of Art); Maurizio Cergol (Fincantieri, Trieste); Tony and Liz Clayden; Dr Giuliano Cominardi (Fincantieri archives, Trieste); Anthony Cooke (Carmania Press, London); Desmond Cox (Snowbow Productions); Sarah Douglas (The Cruise Portfolio); Jennifer Dunn; Matthew Elgie (Swan Hellenic); Sarah Falkingham (Siren PR); Fincantieri at Trieste, Monfalcone and Genoa; Joe and Jeanne Farcus; Iina and Mauri Forsblom; Anne Gleave (Curator of Photographic Archives, Maritime Archives and Library, Merseyside Maritime Museum); Luci Gosling (*The Illustrated London News* Picture Library); Chas Halsey and Ken Pearson (Focal Point); Vicky Hayes (National Maritime Museum); Julian Honer (Merrell Publishing, London); Ceri James and Katherine Ellworthy (The Advertising Archives, London); Ian Johnston (Glasgow School of Art); Elizabeth Kerr (Camera Press, London); Petteri Kummala; Kvaerner-Masa Yards, Helsinki; Angela Lauf (Parfums Jean Patou, Paris); David and Mary Alice Lowenthal; Claire Lyng and Maureen Watry (University of Liverpool Special Collections); Surinder Manku (Royal Caribbean International/Celebrity Cruises); Lisa Moore (David Moore Archive, Sydney); Alison Morgan (Dudson Museum); Gael Newton (Senior Curator of Photography, Australian National Gallery, Canberra); John Noble (index); Sue Parker (Associate Publisher/Editor, *Cruise International*, London); Paolo Piccione; Stephen Rabson and Lizzie Goddard (P&O Archives, London); Kate Selley (Beth Cooper Public Relations); Richard Seville; Tony Smith (World Ship Society); David Trevor-Jones; Marika Vecchiatini (Costa Cruises, Genoa); Sylvia Warren; Peter Wood (Racing Teapots).

This book is for Joe and for Jeanne.

Picture credits

Individual picture captions identify the companies for which items (memorabilia, brochures, etc.) were originally produced. Other sources and copyright information are listed below.

The author and publishers would like to thank all the companies, individuals and photographers whose work is reproduced. In all cases, every effort has been made to contact the copyright holders, but should there be any omissions the publishers would be pleased to insert the appropriate acknowledgement in any subsequent edition of this book.

Peter Quartermaine Collection (6, 23, 27 right, 34 left, 39 left, 42 bottom, 46, 57, 90 bottom, 95, 108, 109, 113, 122 top, 126, 127 top left, 128 bottom right, 137); **Bruce Peter Collection** (39 right, 54, 81, 107 bottom, 110 bottom, 111, 114 bottom right, 138–39, 141); **Bruce Peter/Ingrid Guse** (70 top); **Clive Harvey Collection** (10, 16, 26, 28, 29, 31 top, 32 top, 33, 45 top, 50, 52, 53, 55, 56, 70 bottom, 73 top/bottom left, 75 right, 76, 80, 84 top left/top right, 87, 92 right, 93, 94, 97 top left/bottom right, 114 top left/top right/bottom centre, 115, 124–25, 127 top right); **Laurence Dunn Collection** (31 bottom left/bottom right, 48–49); © Joe Farcus (106 top); **Albert Novelli Collection** (103); **Paolo Piccione Collection** (105); © David Trevor-Jones (128 bottom left); © Disney Cruise Line (62/63, 133); **Dudson Pottery/P&O Cruises** (89 bottom right); **Snowbow Productions** [www.snowbow.co.uk] (112 top); **Courtesy of Mattel** (116); **Courtesy of Parfums Jean Patou, Paris** 113; **Courtesy of Carnival Cruise Lines** (12, 13, 20, 21, 77 left, 78, 79, 96, 97 top, 110 top, 116, 122 bottom, 123); © **Laurence King Publishing** [photos: Fredrika Lökholm and Martin Slivka] (42 bottom, 51, 112 top, 113, 116, 122 top]; © P&O **Archives** (1, 8, 9, 11, 14, 15, 25, 30, 35, 36 top, 37, 42 top, 44, 59, 60, 61, 68, 71, 72, 73 bottom right, 74, 75 left, 86, 88, 89 top, 90 top, 91, 141, 142]; **Courtesy of P&O Cruises** (2–3, 17, 22, 66, 83, 84 bottom, 85, 134, 135, 136 bottom); **Courtesy of Princess Cruises** (67, 128 top, 129); **Courtesy of Royal Caribbean International** (84 top left/top right, 132); **Courtesy of easyCruise** (117, 118, 119, 136 top); **Courtesy of Star Cruises** (58, 77 right, 82, 130, 131); © **Advertising Archives** (43, 69, 101, 114 bottom left); © **Camera Press London** (18, 19 [photo: David Moore], 24 [photo: Francis Goodman], 34 right [photo: Francis Goodman], 40 [photo: Gerald Murison], 41 [photo: David Linton], 65 top [photo: Benoit Gysembergh], 65 (bottom), 99 [photo: Van Rhoon], 104 [photo: Charles Ira Sachs], 140 [photo: Ray Hamilton], 142 [photo: David Linton], 143 [photo: Loomis Dean]); © **Fincantieri, Trieste** (106 bottom); **Courtesy of the University of Liverpool Library** (47 [ref. D42/PR2/1/62/D2], 98 [ref. D42/PR2/1/47/F14]); **Courtesy of National Museums of Liverpool (Merseyside Maritime Museum)** [photos: Stewart Bale] (100, 102); **Courtesy of Lloyd Werft, Bremerhaven** (64); **Courtesy of Southampton Arts and Heritage Services** (45 bottom, 48 left, 49 right, 107 top, 112 left, 114 top centre); **Courtesy of The Mitchell Wolfson Jr. Collection, The Wolfsonian-Florida International University** (27 left, 32 bottom, 36 bottom left/bottom right, 38, 89 bottom left, 92 left); **Courtesy of The World** (120, 121).

Bibliography

Books

There are several paperback guides to selecting a cruise, updated regularly.

Bathe, Basil W., *Seven Centuries of Sea Travel, From the Crusaders to the Cruises* (Portland House, 1973)

Baul, Patrick J., *Half a Century of Cruise Ships in Saint-Nazaire* (Coop Breizh, 2003)

Brendon, Piers, *Thomas Cook: 150 Years of Popular Tourism* (Secker and Warburg, 1991)

Burgess, Jacqueline and Gold, John R., *Geography, The Media and Popular Culture* (Croom Helm, 1985)

Cartwright, Roger and Harvey, Clive, *Cruise Britannia* (Tempus, 2004)

Cooke, Anthony, *Liners and Cruise Ships: Some Notable Smaller Vessels, vol. 1* (Carmania Press, 1996)

Coons, Lorraine and Varias, Alexander, *Tourist Third Cabin: Steamship Travel in the Interwar Years* (Palgrave, 2003)

Cudahy, Brian, *The Cruise Ship Phenomenon in North America* (Cornell Maritime Press, 2001)

Dawson, Phillip, *Cruise Ships: An Evolution in Design* (Conway Maritime Press, 2000)

——, *British Superliners of the Sixties* (Conway Maritime Press, 1990)

Dickinson, Bob and Vladimir, Andy,

Selling the Sea: An Inside Look at the Cruise Industry (Wiley, 1997)

Eliseo, Maurizio and Piccione, Paolo, *The Costa Liners* (Carmania Press, 1997)

Frisby, David *Fragments of Modernity* (Polity Press, 1985)

Graves, John, *Waterline: Images from the Golden Age of Cruising* (National Maritime Museum, 2004)

Kohler, Peter C., *The Lido Fleet* (Seadragon Press, 1998)

Maxtone-Graham, John, *Liners to the Sun* (Macmillan 1985)

Metz, Tracy, *Fun! Leisure and Landscape* (Nai Publishers, 2002)

Miller, William H., *The Cruise Ships* (Conway Maritime Press, 1988)

——, *Modern Cruise Ships, 1965–1990: A Photographic Record* (Dover Publications Inc., 1992)

Mitchell, Don, *Cultural Geography: A Critical Introduction* (Blackwell, 2000)

O'Brien, Martin, *Travel in 'Vogue'* (Macdonald Futura, 1981)

Peter, Bruce, *Passenger Liners Scandinavian Style* (Carmania Press, 2004)

Quartermaine, Peter, *Building on the Sea: Form and Meaning in Modern Ship Architecture* (Academy Editions/National Maritime Museum, 1996)

Raban, Jonathan, *Introduction to The Oxford Book of the Sea* (Oxford, 1992)

Ulrich, Kurt, *Monarchs of the Sea: The Great Ocean Liners* (Tauris Parke, 1997)

Urry, John, *The Tourist Gaze: Leisure and Travel in Contemporary Societies* (Nottingham Trent University TCS series, 1990)

Venturi, Robert, Scott-Brown, Denise and Izenour, Stephen, *Learning from Las Vegas: The Forgotten Symbolism of Architectural Form* (MIT Press, 1972)

Withey, Lynne, *Grand Tours and Cook's Tours: A History of Leisure Travel 1750–1915* (Aurum Press, 1997)

Journals and articles

Anderson, Sir Colin, 'The Interior Design of Passenger Ships', *Journal of the Royal Society of Arts* (London, May 1966) pp. 477–93

Casson, Sir Hugh, 'A Ship is an Island', *The Architectural Review* (London, June 1969) pp. 399–408

Payne, Stephen, 'The Evolution of the Modern Cruise Liner', *The Naval Architect* (London, May 1990) pp. 163–88

Peter, Bruce, 'Identity Onboard' in Fladmark, J.M. (ed), *Heritage and Identity: The Shaping of the Nations of the North* (Donhead, 2001)

Quartermaine, Peter, 'Designing an Experience: The Cruise Ships of Joe Farcus', in *Design Process Progress Practice* (Design Museum, 1999) pp. 127–35

——, 'Passengers at Sea', *The Conway History of Seafaring in the Twentieth Century* (Conway Maritime Press, 2000) pp. 151–67

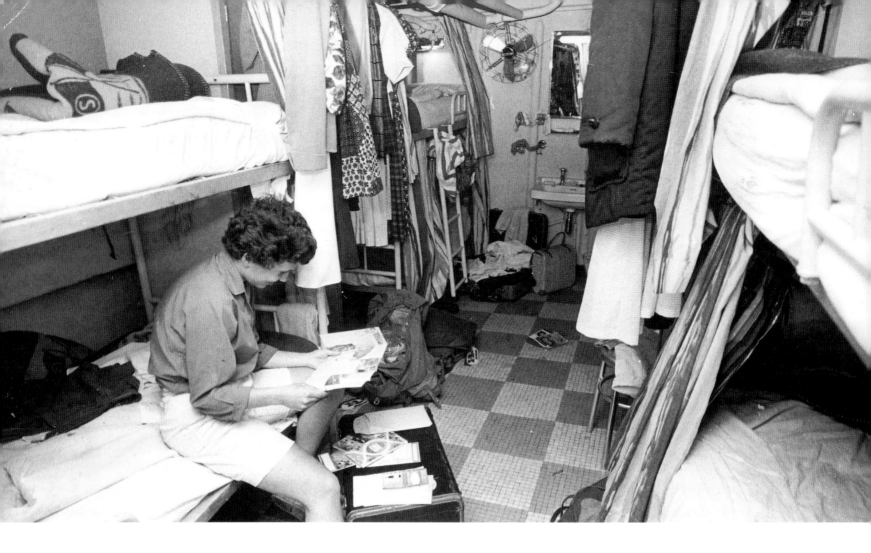

ABOVE Student digs at sea, probably in the 1950s or 1960s, aboard a large transatlantic liner: 'One of the low-cost cabins for girls.' Cheap multiple cabins such as this were often located below the waterline (notice the large fan), and were akin to crew accommodation. Still, the chaos is friendly and, several decks above, there always lies a great expanse of open wooden deck.

FACING Private view. The Andy Warhol bar aboard *The Atlantis*, private yacht of Greek shipping tycoon Stavros Niarchos (1908–1996): 'Each of the twelve guests suites is also named after a different artist: for example, the Dali Suite, the Poliakoff Suite, the Klee Suite and the Van Velde Suite.' From P&O's 1904 'steam yacht' *Vectis* to 'The Yachts of Seabourn' today, the term 'yacht' spells luxury and exclusivity. Though such yachts remain the pleasure objects and status symbols for the super-rich, they feed the aspirations of all who take cruises.

ABOVE Deck chairs being put to energetic use in their natural habitat. A sunny deck, the gentle sound of the ship's wake, and a healthy sea breeze: these elements retain their appeal, despite all the new-fangled entertainment offered by modern ships. This is cruising in the Mediterranean in 1965, classic P&O-style, on the 1961 *Canberra*.

D8